DATE DUE

11-08			
OCT 2 8 2011			
NOV 16 2011			
12/12/13			
DE 2 5 13			
11/19/14			
NOV 3 0 2014			

1st EDITION

Perspectives on Diseases and Disorders

Learning Disabilities

Clay Farris Naff
Book Editor

PERSPECTIVES
On Diseases & Disorders

GALE
CENGAGE Learning

Detroit • New York • San Francisco • New Haven, Conn • Waterville, Maine • London

Christine Nasso, *Publisher*
Elizabeth Des Chenes, *Managing Editor*

© 2010 Greenhaven Press, a part of Gale, Cengage Learning

Gale and Greenhaven Press are registered trademarks used herein under license.

For more information, contact:
Greenhaven Press
27500 Drake Rd.
Farmington Hills, MI 48331-3535
Or you can visit our Internet site at gale.cengage.com

For product information and technology assistance, contact us at

Gale Customer Support, 1-800-877-4253
For permission to use material from this text or product, submit all requests online at www.cengage.com/permissions

Further permissions questions can be e-mailed to permissionrequest@cengage.com

Articles in Greenhaven Press anthologies are often edited for length to meet page requirements. In addition, original titles of these works are changed to clearly present the main thesis and to explicitly indicate the author's opinion. Every effort is made to ensure that Greenhaven Press accurately reflects the original intent of the authors. Every effort has been made to trace the owners of copyrighted material.

Cover image copyright © BSIP/Phototake—All rights reserved.

LIBRARY OF CONGRESS CATALOGING-IN-PUBLICATION DATA

Learning disabilities / Clay Farris Naff, book editor.
   p. cm. -- (Perspectives on diseases and disorders)
  Includes bibliographical references and index.
  ISBN 978-0-7377-5001-0 (hardcover)
  1. Learning disabilities--Popular works. I. Naff, Clay Farris.
  RJ506.L4L34 2010
  618.92'85889--dc22
                                  2010012619

Printed in the United States of America
1 2 3 4 5 6 7 14 13 12 11 10

CONTENTS

CHAPTER 2 Controversies Concerning Learning Disabilities

FOREWORD

"Medicine, to produce health, has to examine disease."
—Plutarch

Independent research on a health issue is often the first
step to complement discussions with a physician. But
locating accurate, well-organized, understandable medical information can be a challenge. A simple Internet search
on terms such as "cancer" or "diabetes," for example, re-
turns an intimidating number of results. Sifting through the
results can be daunting, particularly when some of the information is inconsistent or even contradictory. The Greenhaven Press series Perspectives on Diseases and Disorders
offers a solution to the often overwhelming nature of researching diseases and disorders.

From the clinical to the personal, titles in the Perspectives on Diseases and Disorders series provide students and other researchers with authoritative, accessible
information in unique anthologies that include basic
information about the disease or disorder, controversial
aspects of diagnosis and treatment, and first-person ac-
counts of those impacted by the disease. The result is a
well-rounded combination of primary and secondary
sources that, together, provide the reader with a better
understanding of the disease or disorder.

Each volume in Perspectives on Diseases and Disorders
explores a particular disease or disorder in detail. Material
for each volume is carefully selected from a wide range of
sources, including encyclopedias, journals, newspapers, non-
fiction books, speeches, government documents, pamphlets,
organization newsletters, and position papers. Articles in the
first chapter provide an authoritative, up-to-date overview that covers symptoms, causes and effects, treatments,

cures, and medical advances. The second chapter presents a substantial number of opposing viewpoints on controversial treatments and other current debates relating to the volume topic. The third chapter offers a variety of personal perspectives on the disease or disorder. Patients, doctors, caregivers, and loved ones represent just some of the voices found in this narrative chapter.

Each Perspectives on Diseases and Disorders volume also includes:

- An **annotated table of contents** that provides a brief summary of each article in the volume.
- An **introduction** specific to the volume topic.
- Full-color **charts and graphs** to illustrate key points, concepts, and theories.
- Full-color **photos** that show aspects of the disease or disorder and enhance textual material.
- **"Fast Facts"** that highlight pertinent additional statistics and surprising points.
- A **glossary** providing users with definitions of important terms.
- A **chronology** of important dates relating to the disease or disorder.
- An annotated list of **organizations to contact** for students and other readers seeking additional information.
- A **bibliography** of additional books and periodicals for further research.
- A detailed **subject index** that allows readers to quickly find the information they need.

Whether a student researching a disorder, a patient recently diagnosed with a disease, or an individual who simply wants to learn more about a particular disease or disorder, a reader who turns to Perspectives on Diseases and Disorders will find a wealth of information in each volume that offers not only basic information, but also vigorous debate from multiple perspectives.

INTRODUCTION

When Chuck was a boy he struggled to read. Neither his teachers nor his parents had any idea that a specific condition—dyslexia—was responsible. They just leaned on him to try harder. That did not work. He managed to scrape through high school, but when he got to college he hit the wall.

"The first two years I struggled . . . I flunked English twice. They just passed me through the third time," Chuck recalls. "I got an F in French. I had a tough enough time with the first language. When I came out of public high school I thought I could charm my teachers. I found out in college I couldn't."[1]

Eventually, by focusing on economics, Chuck managed to graduate and went on to prove in spectacular fashion that learning disabilities do not equate with stupidity or laziness.

Chuck is Charles Schwab, the founder of a financial services empire that bears his name. For all his success, however, Schwab admits that he still cannot read very well, and whenever possible he listens to recorded books rather than try to read them. His learning disorder is something he has had to learn to live with.

That is true for millions of Americans and millions more worldwide. While no precise figures are available, experts estimate that about one in twenty children suffers a learning disability. That amounts to more than 3 million children in the United States. Like Schwab, however, more may be undiagnosed.

Learning disabilities are neurological disorders—problems in brain wiring—that cause specific difficulties

Charles Schwab, founder of the Charles Schwab Corporation, overcame a learning disability to found a highly successful brokerage firm. (Jim Young/Reuters/Landov)

for certain types of learning. Children with learning disabilities may be as smart as their peers—or even smarter. But they cannot learn in the same way. The have difficulty with reading, writing, spelling, reasoning, recalling and/or organizing information. A learning disability cannot be cured—not so far, at any rate. However, it can be accommodated. With the right learning environment, technology, and support, children with learning disabilities can succeed in school and go on to a successful career, as Schwab has proved. Schwab and his wife have created a foundation to help children with learning disabilities.

Learning disabilities come in many varieties, and they do not always make themselves easy to spot. You cannot usually tell by looking that a person has a learning disability. That can make diagnosing one quite challenging. Mistakes are made: Some children with psychiatric disorders are put on medications more suitable for treating a learning disorder, and vice versa. Getting the diagnosis right is critical to helping the individual cope with his or her learning disability. The two most common learning disabilities require radically different responses.

Dyslexia, which afflicts Schwab, also affects millions of other Americans. It results in profound difficulty in reading. The origins of dyslexia are still not entirely understood, but experts believe it results from a difficulty in associating sounds with parts of words. For many dyslexics, the best work-around is to make use of recorded books.

Attention deficit hyperactivity disorder (ADHD), the other leading learning disability, results in an inability to concentrate long enough to learn. It is most often treated with drug therapies. For many young people, Ritalin or a related pharmaceutical works well to control their hyperactivity and allow them to concentrate on learning.

People with dyscalculia have trouble processing simple numerical information. Reading a clock face may be challenging. Adding a column of numbers may prove impossible. There are no cures for such disabilities, but there are some coping mechanisms that people can be taught.

Some people have nonverbal learning disabilities that make it hard to process what they see. They may have trouble making sense of visual symbols or decoding an image from its background.

Emotional-social disorders can also interfere with learning. Until recently, it was widely believed that children with so-called autism spectrum disorders were mentally retarded, but recent research has shown that this is often not the case. They simply cannot learn or communicate their learning in the same way as mainstream children. Some autistic children display what are called savant talents—the ability to learn one particular skill at a level far higher than what might be expected for their age. However, they are incapable of normal social interaction and frequently find the atmosphere of a standard classroom totally disorienting.

Children with autism spectrum disorders (ASDs)—a range of social integration syndromes and symptoms that often interfere with learning—need special learning environments and understanding, well-trained teachers. Given those, they are often capable of learning, sometimes with outstanding results. Education systems, however, are all too often unprepared to meet those needs.

A mother in England who ran into brick walls while trying to get appropriate educational services for her two ASD sons went to extraordinary lengths to meet their needs. She and her husband started a school especially for children with ASD.

"A total of 26 special schools, within an hour's drive of where my family and I lived, turned down applications for my boys' placements," Anna Kennedy recalls. "Doors were being shut in our faces on a regular basis and we hardly knew where to turn. . . . Faced with the difficulty of finding anywhere that would provide educational support for my boys, and our inability to find suitable childcare for children on the autistic spectrum in our locality, we took drastic measures."[2]

She and her husband mortgaged their house, raised funds, recruited special education teachers, and launched their school. Soon it was in high demand by parents with children whose disorders made it impossible for them to learn in a standard school environment. She recently published a memoir about her sons' education with the apt title *Not Stupid*.

If one thing has been learned about learning disorders in recent decades, it is this: There are no simple answers. No magical cures. No one-size-fits-all accommodations. But given the right learning environment, the right training for teachers, and the right technology to support them, students with learning disabilities can succeed.

This last item, technology, has made an enormous difference. For dyslexics, recorded books make all the difference. Not long ago, recorded books were hard to come by and cumbersome, as they would be divided up among many cassette tapes. Now, with the proliferation of MP3 players and access to the Internet, the only difficulty is making sure that required texts are available in recorded form.

Many children with ADHD respond well to drug therapy. Taking the correct dosage helps them to relax and concentrate. Not all children can tolerate the amphetamine-like drugs, and regrettably some youths abuse the drugs, often to their detriment.

Children with autism spectrum disorders often improve dramatically when they are exposed to special learning environments with trained teachers.
(© Phototake Inc./Alamy)

New technological aids for those with learning disabilities are being devised all the time. A more fundamental need, however, is respect. All too often, children with learning disabilities are mocked in school, sometimes even by teachers.

Looking back on his own frustrating experience, Charles Schwab says, "Some kids feel like they're stupid. I want them to know that they're not. They just learn differently. Once they understand that and have the tools to learn in their individual way, then they can feel good about themselves."

Notes

1. Quoted in Todd Pitt, "Charles Schwab Didn't Let Dyslexia Stop Him," *USA Today*, November 10, 2003. www.usatoday.com/money/companies/management/2003-11-10-schwab_x.htm.
2. Anna Kennedy, "Not Stupid: One Woman's Fight for Her Sons' (Special) Education," *Age of Autism*, August 22, 2009. www.ageofautism.com/2009/08/not-stupid-one-womans-fight-for-her-sons-special-education.html.

CHAPTER 1

Understanding Learning Disabilities

Overview of Learning Disabilities

Paula Ford-Martin and Rebecca Frey

Learning disorders are a major stumbling block in education. According to the following selection at least 2 million youngsters in America have learning disorders. The children are not intellectually impaired, the authors explain. Their learning disorders affect specific abilities to take in, process, and store information. Thus, children with learning disorders typically perform well below what their IQs would predict. Learning disorders occur in a variety of basic skills, including reading, writing, and mathematics. Diagnosis can be tricky, but once a disorder is identified a unique plan for the child's education can be drawn up to counter its effects. Medical writer Paula Ford-Martin and researcher Rebecca Frey are frequent contributors to the *Gale Encyclopedia of Medicine* and similar publications.

Photo on previous page. No accurate statistics can be found on the number of children affected by learning disabilities because no universally accepted tests or assessment standards exist. (**Anabella Bluesky/Photo Researchers, Inc.**)

Learning disorders are academic difficulties experienced by children and adults of average to above-average intelligence. People with learning disorders

SOURCE: Paula Ford-Martin and Rebecca Frey, *Gale Encyclopedia of Medicine.* Farmington Hills, MI: Gale, 2006. Copyright © 2006 Gale, Cengage Learning. Reproduced by permission of Gale, a part of Cengage Learning.

have difficulty with reading, writing, mathematics, or a combination of the three. These difficulties significantly interfere with academic achievement or daily living.

Learning disorders, or disabilities, affect approximately 2 million children between the ages of six and 17 (5% of public school children), although some experts think the figure may be as high as 15%. These children have specific impairments in acquiring, retaining, and processing information. Standardized tests place them well below their IQ range in their area of difficulty. The three main types of learning disorders are reading disorders, mathematics disorders, and disorders of written expression. The male: female ratio for learning disorders is about 5:1.

Reading Disorders

Reading disorders are the most common type of learning disorder. Children with reading disorders have difficulty recognizing and interpreting letters and words (dyslexia). They aren't able to recognize and decode the sounds and syllables (phonetic structure) behind written words and language in general. This condition lowers accuracy and comprehension in reading.

Mathematics Disorders

Children with mathematics disorders (dyscalculia) have problems recognizing and counting numbers correctly. They have difficulty using numbers in everyday settings. Mathematics disorders are typically diagnosed in the first few years of elementary school when formal teaching of numbers and basic math concepts begins. Children with mathematics disorders usually have a co-existing reading disorder, a disorder of written expression, or both.

Disorders of Written Expression

Disorders of written expression typically occur in combination with reading disorders or mathematics disorders

Children suffering from dyscalculia have problems recognizing and counting numbers correctly. (© vario images GmbH & Co.KG/Alamy)

or both. The condition is characterized by difficulty with written compositions (dysgraphia). Children with this type of learning disorder have problems with spelling, punctuation, grammar, and organizing their thoughts in writing.

Causes and Symptoms

Learning disorders are thought to be caused by neurological abnormalities that trigger impairments in the regions of the brain that control visual and language processing and attention and planning. These traits may be genetically linked. Children from families with a history of learning disorders are more likely to develop disorders themselves. In 2003 a team of Finnish researchers reported finding a candidate gene for developmental dyslexia on human chromosome 15q21.

PERSPECTIVES ON DISEASES AND DISORDERS

Learning difficulties may also be caused by such medical conditions as a traumatic brain injury or brain infections such as encephalitis or meningitis.

The defining symptom of a learning disorder is academic performance that is markedly below a child's age and grade capabilities and measured IQ. Children with a reading disorder may confuse or transpose words or letters and omit or add syllables to words. The written homework of children with disorders of written expression is filled with grammatical, spelling, punctuation, and organizational errors. The child's handwriting is often extremely poor. Children with mathematical disorders are often unable to count in the correct sequence, to name numbers, and to understand numerical concepts.

Identifying Learning Disorders

Problems with vision or hearing, mental disorders (depression, attention-deficit/hyperactivity disorder), mental retardation, cultural and language differences, and inadequate teaching may be mistaken for learning disorders or complicate a diagnosis. A comprehensive medical, psychological, and educational assessment is critical to making a clear and correct diagnosis.

A child thought to have a learning disorder should undergo a complete medical examination to rule out an organic cause. If none is found, a psychoeducational assessment should be performed by a psychologist, psychiatrist, neurologist, neuropsychologist, or learning specialist. A complete medical, family, social, and educational history is compiled from existing medical and school records and from interviews with the child and the child's parents and teachers. A series of written and verbal tests are then given to the child to evaluate his or her cognitive and intellectual functioning. Commonly used tests include the

FAST FACT

There are no universally accepted tests, assessment batteries, or standards for identifying children with learning disabilities. This leads to widely varying statistics about the incidence and distribution of learning disabilities.

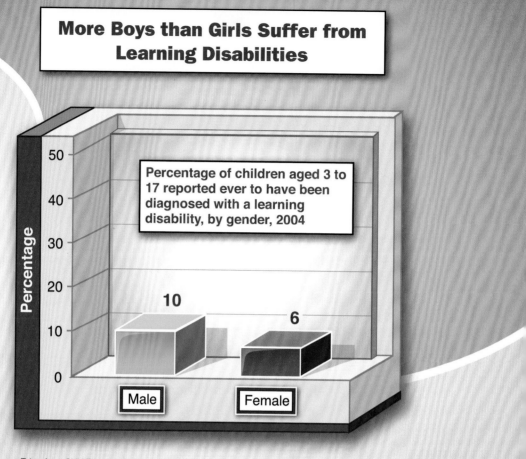

More Boys than Girls Suffer from Learning Disabilities

Percentage of children aged 3 to 17 reported ever to have been diagnosed with a learning disability, by gender, 2004

Taken from: Child Trends DataBank. www.childtrendsdatabank.org/figures/65-Figure-1.gif.

Wechsler Intelligence Scale for Children (WISC-III), the Woodcock-Johnson Psychoeducational Battery, the Peabody Individual Achievement Test–Revised (PIAT-R) and the California Verbal Learning Test (CVLT). Federal legislation mandates that this testing is free of charge within the public school system. . . .

Tailoring Education to the Child

Once a learning disorder has been diagnosed, an individual education plan (IEP) is developed for the child in question. IEPs are based on psychoeducational test findings. They provide for annual retesting to measure a child's progress. Learning-disordered students may receive special instruction within a regular general education class or they may be taught in a special education or learning center for a portion of the day.

Common strategies for the treatment of reading disorders focus first on improving a child's recognition of the sounds of letters and language through phonics training. Later strategies focus on comprehension, retention, and study skills. Students with disorders of written expression are often encouraged to keep journals and to write with a computer keyboard instead of a pencil. Instruction for students with mathematical disorders emphasizes real-world uses of arithmetic, such as balancing a checkbook or comparing prices.

Sensory Confusion Contributes to Dyslexia

Jean Mercer

A common perception about dyslexia is that those who suffer from it cannot properly see the letters or words on a page. However, in the following selection psychologist Jean Mercer cites evidence that this is not the case. If a person consistently sees a letter reversed, it will make no difference to them, she argues. Their visual relationship with that letter will be the same. Rather than vision, Mercer says, researchers are homing in on auditory problems as the likely cause of dyslexia. Slow or faulty processing of the sounds of words or their components may make it hard for a child to learn to associate them correctly with letters. Studies suggest that this is the key contributor to dyslexia.

Mercer received her doctorate in general experimental psychology from Brandeis University. She has taught developmental psychology in college and is the author of a textbook on infant development and of *Understanding Attachment*, a general-interest book about early emotional development.

Preschool children often show confusion about letters of the alphabet. They write them backward or upside-down and don't seem to care about the differences we point out between their productions and the standard version. As they get older, some children continue to make the same mistakes, and their efforts to read are confused as they ignore the order of letters or even of words. After a few years of schooling, these children's continuing difficulties with reading are often classified as dyslexia. Dyslexic children may get behind in other subjects as well, because they are expected to gain knowledge by the very reading skills they are struggling to develop. It's no wonder that so many efforts have been made to understand dyslexia and to treat it effectively.

In the past, a common explanation offered for dyslexia was that these poor readers "saw backwards" and therefore reversed letters both when they read and when they wrote. It's hardly possible that people would "see backwards" only when looking at print, and if they "saw backwards" all the time it would certainly be apparent in their daily behavior. For example, if someone's vision reverses left and right, we'd expect that person to reach to the left for a doorknob that was actually on the right, or to find it impossible to look at and button a shirt with buttons on the left and holes on the right. But we don't see people with these problems.

Not Inverted Sight

In addition, logic tells us that if someone always saw left and right reversed, he or she could still learn to recognize letters. If such a hypothetical person wanted to write a letter, he or she would make it look correct to the rest of us, because only in that way could it appear in its normal or "reversed" position from the reverser's viewpoint. (This argument is similar to the logic that refutes the "El Greco fallacy" in the study of

Dyslexics often confuse the letters *p, b, d,* and *q,* as well as *m, w, n,* and *u,* making reading difficult.
(Emmeline Watkins/ Photo Researchers, Inc.)

art history.[1] Consistent reversal of shapes would make no difference to reading or writing, and a person who experienced "flips" from one orientation to another would surely mention this or show it behaviorally.

All this suggests that dyslexia probably has little to do with vision itself. But learning to read involves another critical sense: hearing. A first step in reading is to associate the shape of a letter (grapheme) with the sound or sounds it represents (one or more phonemes). A child who has difficulty in processing speech sounds will also have trouble associating those sounds with shapes.

Speech Sounds Are Complex

One of the difficulties in processing and recognizing speech sounds is that these are not simple patterns of sound waves—even though they seem that way to a listener. We hear a speech sound as if it were a unit of

---

1. The El Greco Fallacy arises from the mistaken belief of some that the painter El Greco had a vision defect that made him see people as tall and thin. In reality, it was an artistic choice he made in his paintings.

stimulation, quickly begun, quickly finished, and of uniform characteristics from beginning to end. However, a speech sound involves complex patterns of sound waves, often varying a great deal from onset to finish. These sound wave changes happen extremely fast, and the auditory areas of the brain have to be very quick to respond to them. If the response is slow, the sound is all over before processing is well under way. A person who is abnormally slow in processing speech sounds could be expected to have trouble connecting the poorly-perceived sound with a specific letter of the alphabet. (Incidentally, such a person would have "normal hearing" in the sense of being able to detect very soft sounds; the problem would be not in detecting the sounds but in identifying them.)

Effective Listening Required

In a recent article in *Science*, John Gabrieli described some of the difficulties dyslexic children have with "phonological awareness"—the ability to detect and identify not only different sounds but the order they appear in. For example, they have trouble listening to words and deciding which ones start with the same sound (does "hat" start with the same sound as "hot" or as "bat"?). This shows that the problem with reading is not simply a matter of deciding what a letter looks like; effective listening needs to be achieved before reading can be done fluently. However, Gabrieli also pointed out some research showing subtle differences in dyslexics' visual abilities, although no problems that would appear on any ordinary test of vision.

FAST FACT

Conductive hearing loss in early childhood, caused by ear infections or other obstructive problems in the ear, is the main cause of dyslexia.

Gabrieli and some co-workers have shown that a computer-game approach can help dyslexic children improve their ability for rapid auditory processing. However, it is not clear how directly this change contributes

Dyslexic Children Have Trouble Identifying Off-Key Musical Notes

Dyslexic children take slightly longer than nondyslexic children to recognize that a musical note is off key. Because dyslexics are slower to identify off-key notes, they may be slower to relate sounds to words.

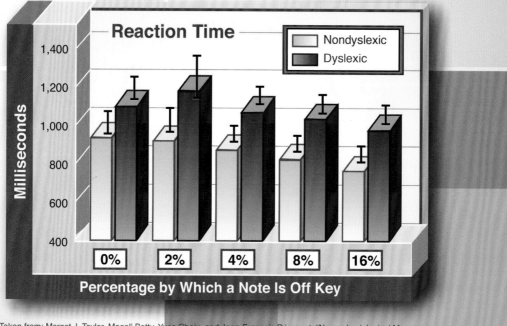

Taken from: Margot J. Taylor, Magali Batty, Yves Chaix, and Jean-François Démonet, "Neurophysiological Measures and Developmental Dyslexia: Auditory Segregation Analysis," *Current Psychology Letters*, no. 10, vol. 1, 2003. http://cpl.revues.org/index101.html.

to improved reading. Specific instruction can be helpful, but it is expensive and should be directed to children who are most at risk for reading problems. An important task for the future is to develop methods of identifying these children early and intervening before they are far behind educationally.

Attention Deficit Hyperactivity Disorder Disrupts Learning

Ruth D. Nass and Fern Leventhal

Attention deficit hyperactivity disorder (ADHD) is among the most common of learning disorders. In the following selection two experts, Ruth D. Nass and Fern Leventhal, address some of the basic questions about ADHD. They explain that the disorder is characterized by impulsive and inattentive behavior that falls outside the normal range for a child of a given age. This imbalance, in turn, can be traced to the child's genes. Thus, the condition can be exacerbated by parental mismanagement, but its causes are not environmental. Rather, ADHD results from biochemical imbalances in the child's brain, they state. It most often becomes apparent in elementary school.

Nass is a professor of clinical pediatric neurology at the New York University Medical Center. Leventhal is a clinical neuropsychologist at the New York University Medical Center and the New York State Psychiatric Institute.

SOURCE: Ruth D. Nass and Fern Leventhal, *100 Questions and Answers About Your Child's Attention Deficit Hyperactivity Disorder.* Copyright © 2005 by Jones and Bartlett Publishers, Sudbury, MA. www.jbpub.com. All rights reserved. Reprinted with permission.

A ttention deficit hyperactivity disorder (ADHD) is a disorder in which a child displays hyperactive, impulsive, and/or inattentive behavior that is age-inappropriate. ADHD is a result of an atypical chemical balance in the brain, which means that ADHD is a physical problem, not an emotional problem. Outside factors, such as poor parenting, a chaotic home situation, divorce, or school stresses may affect how the symptoms come to light, but they do not cause ADHD. In order to diagnose ADHD (according to the *Diagnostic*

Attention Deficit Hyperactivity Disorder (ADHD) in Children

The incidence of ADHD in children varies with family structure, from highest in single-mother homes to lowest in two-parent homes.

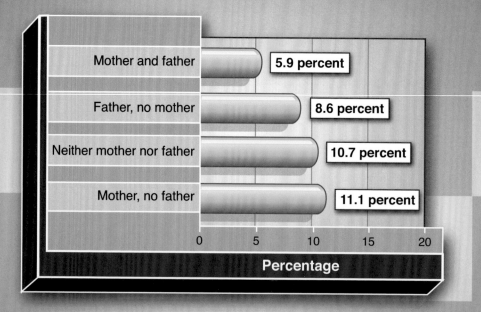

	Percentage
Mother and father	5.9 percent
Father, no mother	8.6 percent
Neither mother nor father	10.7 percent
Mother, no father	11.1 percent

Taken from: Centers for Disease Control and Prevention, "Summary Health Statistics for U.S. Children: National Health Interview Survey, 2006," 2007, p. 18.

and Statistical Manual of Mental Disorders, Fourth Edition, Text Revision [DSM-IV-TR]), problems of inattention, hyperactivity, or impulsivity must interfere with a child's functioning in at least two settings (home, school, or social situations). In addition, the guidelines state that at least some symptoms must have been present before the age of 7 years.

A Widespread Disorder

ADHD is quite common; it is conservatively estimated to affect 3% to 5% of school-age children. Some reports suggest that as many as 4% to 8% or even an amazing 10% to 18% of children have ADHD. Thus, somewhere between 2 and 13 million American children have ADHD. Put another way, on the average, at least one child in every classroom has ADHD. ADHD resulted in almost 10 million physician visits in 2001.

Approximately 60% of children with ADHD have symptoms that persist into adulthood. This means that about 4% of the U.S. adult population, or close to 8 million adults, have ADHD. However, as ADHD is a behavioral disorder, still lacking a specific biological marker, estimates of its frequency can be affected by a number of factors.

The method for making the diagnosis most certainly affects the estimated frequency. The current DSM-IV-TR standards, which allow both hyperactive-impulsive and inattentive subtypes, have resulted in higher rates of diagnosis than previous DSM standards, which placed a higher emphasis on hyperactivity as a diagnostic criterion. In other words, the frequency of the diagnosis increases when hyperactivity is not regarded as a necessary characteristic for ADHD diagnosis. The looser the requirements are, the greater the number of individuals included under the diagnostic umbrella.

The estimated frequency of ADHD also depends on who provides the information to make the diagnosis:

ADHD is characterized by impulsive and inattentive behavior that is outside the normal range for children of given ages. (© Bubbles Photolibrary/ Alamy)

parent, teacher, child, or physician. All have their own agendas to report. Teachers are seeing children through the lens of the classroom, where there are specific academic and behavioral expectations. In a class full of children, disruption by a single student can have a ripple effect. On the other hand, in a large class full of children, teachers may not notice the quietly inattentive child. Children may be less aware of their own symptoms. Adolescents, in particular, are notorious for underreporting and minimizing their symptoms. Parents view their children's behavior from the perspective of day-in, day-out living. Their perspective is intensive as well as long term. On the one hand, they may minimize symptoms that they have been living with for years. On the other hand, the behavior seen under the intensive daily lens may make them keenly aware of things that go unnoticed by others. Physicians see children in a rather artificial setting, where the child is the focus of attention and may be on his or her best behavior. Conversely, some children are stressed by a visit to the doctor and demonstrate ADHD-like signs immediately by wandering around the office touching and picking up everything in sight.

The problem of varying perspectives is highlighted in one study that asked parents, teachers, and physicians to rate children with school problems as having or not having ADHD. Results indicated that approximately 10% were rated a unanimous "yes" and 30% a unanimous "no." However, parents, teachers, and physicians disagreed on the diagnosis of almost two-thirds of the children.

Even Quantitative Diagnoses Differ

Studies using quantitative questionnaires to assess the level of agreement between parents, teachers, and children demonstrate more consistency among raters. But the specific questionnaire used affects the level of agreement. Some of the shorter questionnaires tend to diagnose ADHD less frequently because they emphasize hyperactivity and, subsequently, miss the inattentive children. Longer questionnaires, which consider multiple situations in which attention is required, yield greater agreement among raters and are probably more reliable diagnostic tools.

The child's age at evaluation also makes a difference. Younger children tend to have more classic symptoms and more hyperactivity. Thus, the diagnosis is more likely to be made in these younger children than in older inattentive, nonhyperactive children.

ADHD seems to occur with differing frequency in different cultures. For example, ADHD appears to be more common in the United States than in Britain. A large British national study found the prevalence of hyperkinetic disorder (the British term for hyperactivity) to be only 1.4%. In Japan, a study that based diagnosis on an older version of the *DSM* (which places a greater emphasis on hyperactivity for diagnosis) determined that 8% of children in the general population met the standards for ADHD. The frequency of ADHD in two South American countries, Columbia and Venezuela, ranged from 7% to 11%. Studies coming out of Germany suggest a frequency of approximately 16%. The differences could be a reflection of different thresholds for diagnosis between the different cultures or different diagnostic criteria (or both). For example, in Britain, hyperactivity appears to be a more important symptom for diagnosis than in the United States. The variation in frequency could also be a reflection of differing gene pools in these countries, with more ADHD genes in one population than in another. . . .

ADHD Age Spectrum

Most certainly, the disorder affects individuals of all ages. Of the more than 8 million visits for ADHD to community physicians in 1999, 5% were preschoolers, approximately 66% were elementary-school age, 20% were teenagers, and 15% were adults. ADHD, however, is most often diagnosed in elementary school-age children. Some children are diagnosed later during their junior high school and high school years. It is not unusual for individuals to receive their first diagnosis of ADHD as adults. Interestingly, many parents first recognize that *they* have ADHD when it is diagnosed in their child. As this disorder was not diagnosed very frequently years ago, many individuals went through their school years with undiagnosed ADHD. Subsequently, when parents see their children experiencing similar difficulties, they remember their own history, are able to relate, and confirm their own undiagnosed disorder. . . .

Many children do outgrow ADHD. However, the latest data suggest that 50% to 70% of children continue to have some symptoms of ADHD into adolescence, and as many as 50% have persistent ADHD into adulthood. However, even in persistent cases, the number of symptoms decreases during adolescence and usually decreases further in adulthood. From a biological vantage point, the reduction of symptoms probably reflects continuing brain maturation that goes on through adolescence and beyond.

Genes Influence ADHD

You may be aware that many functions in our body, including production of hormones and other body and brain chemicals, are controlled by specific genes—the molecules of DNA that tell our cells how to develop and behave. You may not, however, have a clear idea of how this really works—and the fact is that scientists didn't either until fairly recently. Efforts at mapping the human genome have helped determine some of the genes controlling specific functions, but many genes affect body systems in ways that scientists have yet to figure out. In some cases, multiple genes may be involved in complex interactions to cause an organ or a system to function properly (or improperly, as in the case of ADHD and many other disorders).

> **FAST FACT**
>
> Driving poses special risks for teens with ADHD. In fact teens with ADHD are two to four times more likely to have a car accident than teens without ADHD.

Genetic studies of ADHD have focused largely on genes involved in controlling the neurotransmitter dopamine. This is logical because medications that increase dopamine are effective treatments for ADHD. Furthermore, brain-imaging studies have identified abnormalities in the dopamine-rich frontal and striatal regions in individuals with ADHD. In animal models used to investigate ADHD, "knock-out" mice—mice missing a gene important for increasing dopamine—are hyperactive and do not respond to stimulant treatment. Their dopamine can't be increased in any way, and they remain hyperactive.

At the moment, the gene or genes most likely to cause ADHD involve dopamine regulation. The dopamine transporter (DAT) gene is the prime candidate. This gene regulates the amount of dopamine in the synapse by determining how much dopamine is reabsorbed into the presynaptic neurons. In controls, the dopamine transporter keeps the level of dopamine in the synapse relatively high. In ADHD, the DAT "overfunctions" and lowers the level of synaptic dopamine. Stimulants inhibit DAT. As a result, more dopamine remains in the synapse. Other possible causal genes control postsynaptic dopamine receptors. They affect the sensitivity of the receptors to dopamine. It takes more dopamine to activate the postsynaptic receptors in children with ADHD.

So what does this knowledge mean for treating children with ADHD? First, it may help scientists design better medications for treating ADHD. They can target the cause of the neurotransmitter problem. Second, scientists can work toward treatments, called gene therapy, that correct the genetic abnormalities of conditions like ADHD. Such therapies are a long way off, but they are nonetheless a promising avenue for investigators.

Autism Interferes with Learning

Diana Friedlander

Autism is a condition that interferes with normal social development and interaction. In the following selection Diana Friedlander
describes how autism interferes with learning. Children with autism
have difficulty understanding what is expected of them in a social
environment, she says. They do not pick up cues in the environment
in the way that other children do. They may have an imbalance in
their senses, causing them to pay more attention to one sensory
input than another in ways that may not seem appropriate. Lighting
or ventilation may bother them. Since they have trouble making
social bonds, they often feel anxiety around others. All these challenges can make learning extra difficult. Friedlander offers teachers
ideas about how to structure the classroom environment to make it
as welcoming as possible for a student with autism.

Friedlander, of Ridgefield, Connecticut, is a special education
teacher in elementary education. She is also a doctoral candidate
at Western Connecticut State University.

SOURCE: Diana Friedlander, "Sam Comes to School: Including
Students with Autism in Your Classroom," *Clearing House*, January/
February 2009, pp. 141–43. Copyright © 2009 by Helen Dwight
Reid Educational Foundation. Reproduced with permission of the
Helen Dwight Reid Educational Foundation, published by Heldref
Publications, 1319 Eighteenth Street, NW, Washington, DC 20036-1802.

Sam's first day of school was different from everyone else's. He walked into the brightly lit, cheerful classroom and quickly became engrossed in the faint whirring of an overhead fan. Chewing on his shirtsleeve, he began rocking and humming. His eyes darted from the welcome message the teacher had printed on the board to posters of color words and days of the week and names printed above each cubby, avidly reading each word and trying to make sense of this new world. Whereas most of the children were eager to meet their teacher and classmates, Sam did not notice them or the other adults in the classroom. Sam's autism created an invisible barrier around him, protecting him from the social world of the classroom and allowing him to find comfort in familiar sounds, symbols, and patterns. At times, however, the barrier was not enough and other stimuli sent him into a panicky terror.

Spectrum of Social Disorders

Autism is one of a group of developmental disorders called Autism Spectrum Disorders (ASDs). ASDs include a wide continuum: Autism, Pervasive Development Disorder, Asperger's Syndrome, Fragile X Syndrome, and Obsessive Compulsive Disorder. Researchers are beginning to understand the genetic components of autism, which affects about 1 in 166 children born in the United States. This frequency is put in perspective by the statistical knowledge that only 1 in 800 babies is born with Down Syndrome.

Most children diagnosed with an ASD have difficulty in social areas, such as picking up cues from their environment and the ability to form typical relationships. Language is another area of difficulty. Although children with an ASD may have adequate expressive language, sometimes beyond their years, receptive language may be compromised. Sensory integration is another troublesome spot. Students with an ASD can have difficulty regulating input into their central nervous system, resulting in sensitivity to touch, sound, taste, or smell. Sam once told a story of how he caught a snake after hearing it slither.

When a child is diagnosed with autism, a lack of social or emotional reciprocity in his or her classroom experience causes the most impact. The social aspects of childhood and school come easily to most children, but

Because children with autism spectrum disorders often have difficulties with social interactions, classrooms need to be structured to make them as welcoming as possible. (Burger/Phanie/ Photo Researchers, Inc.)

not to children with autism. Children learn to thrive and grow in their environment by watching and copying others; however, those who have autism often fail to make these social connections. Their isolation causes them to remain inexperienced in a world of comparably savvy children and can make adolescence an unnavigable maze.

Parental Involvement

Teachers slowly come to know their students. In the first few days of class they find out who is an avid reader or a social butterfly, who has the book out and is on the correct page, and who needs their hand held on the way to and from the lunchroom. Find out all you can about your student with autism before he or she arrives in your classroom; this will ease the transition for the student, for you, and for the class. Parents are the most important resource because they know their child best. As with all children, those who have autism are unique. Although they may share some common strengths and weaknesses, each child's individual needs must be evaluated.

Teachers should consider that children with autism are generally rigid in their thinking and behaviors. Typically, once they gain an understanding of a specific concept, they tend to access related information in the confines of that concept. For example, one child learned that a specific pet was called a *dog;* therefore, all pets became known to that child as dogs. This concrete analysis of the world helps them to maintain an orderly and comfortable life with few surprises. Routinization and rituals are common behaviors among some students with autism, as the familiar bears less uncertainty. Often behaviors that are troublesome in school are actually manifestations of uncertainty and lack of order or ritual, which can be frightening to children with autism. Sometimes a child's controlled world may not blend well with the organization you had planned to make your classroom work. A meeting with parents and their child before school begins will give you and the family time to plan for and avoid pitfalls. Parents have a good sense of how their child will react in a given setting. They have developed strategies to make life at home and school work for their child. Brainstorming with them on how to make this transition easy will pay off.

In some cases, easing the transition can be as simple as allowing the child to visit his or her classroom a few times in late summer or setting up a buddy system with a familiar child. Often, you will need to take further steps. For example, a clearly delineated visual schedule, often written out or using drawings or photographs, can help ease the uncertainty of time and transitions by providing advance notice and giving the child with autism a visual cue as to what comes next, thereby increasing his or her comfort level and allowing him or her to internalize the change and respond better. Seeing the chart change or participating in changing the icons helps the child understand and accept change. Students who have relied on this type of system to help structure their early school years can progress to the more sophisticated support of a highly organized day planner or an electronic personal organizer. Parents can provide assistance by predetermining where their child might encounter difficulty throughout the school day and sharing various techniques for addressing these difficulties. Together, you can formulate an environmental support plan to help the child meet daily expectations.

FAST FACT

In 1943 physician Leo Kanner coined the term *autistic* to describe children who seemed unable to relate to themselves or others. The term derives from the root *auto,* for "self."

Implementation of this plan must be consistent or it will add to the child's anxiety level. It must be appropriately designed to meet each child's unique needs; if Sam needs to adapt to a busy cafeteria, he should be taught supportive strategies. This may include bringing comfort foods from home, having a designated seat, being told exactly how much time he has to eat before he is expected to clean up his place, or being assigned a buddy who understands his discomfort and who will model appropriate lunchroom protocol for him until he understands it. . . .

Sensory Overload

A lack of understanding of one's social world along with an unregulated sensory integration system can be anxiety producing. As students grow and mature, they face uncharted territory. These challenges are often met with heightened anxiety and overt behaviors. Temple Grandin, a professor who writes simply and honestly about her own autism, describes an anxiety reducing machine she built at age eighteen that consisted of two heavily padded boards that squeezed along the sides of her body. This machine produced the sensory input she craved and desensitized her overworked nervous system, thus reducing her anxiety.

Children with autism sometimes feel sensory overload in environments in which most people feel comfortable. Overhead lighting, especially fluorescent lights that buzz or flash; noise from fans or air conditioners; the clinking of dishes in the cafeteria down the hall; or a line tapping against a metal flagpole outside can send them into a tailspin. Sensory issues in which the central nervous system craves input may also appear. These children need constant sensory stimulation and may benefit from wearing a weighted vest, having a fidget toy, sitting on an inflated or rice-filled chair cushion, or using an exercise band strung between the front legs of their chair that they can push with their foot or leg. These sensitivities and the strategies for coping with them can influence learning, attention, behavior, and social interaction.

Graduation Rates of High School Students with Autism and Other Impairments, 2006

Number and percentage distribution of students aged 14 to 21 with disabilities served under the Individuals with Disabilities Education Act who exited school, by exit status and type of disability for school year 2005–2006:

Disability	Total number exiting special education	Graduated with diploma (percentage)	Received a certificate of attendance (percentage)	Reached maximum age (percentage)	Died (percentage)
Mental retardation	46,588	36.7	35.5	4.6	0.8
Emotional disturbance	47,519	43.4	9.9	1.2	0.5
Speech or language impairment	8,923	67.3	9.2	0.5	0.2
Multiple disabilities	8,251	43.8	25.6	8.3	3.6
Other health impairment	32,274	63.4	11.7	0.6	0.9
Hearing impairment	4,674	68.7	16.5	1.2	0.3
Orthopedic impairment	3,455	61.7	19.2	3.8	3.6
Visual impairment	1,766	72.1	13.9	1.6	1.1
Autism	4,876	57.1	26.6	6.7	0.5
Deafness/ blindness	150	65.3	14.0	8.7	3.3
Traumatic brain injury	2,246	65.0	16.5	2.9	0.8

Support from parents and a knowledgeable occupational therapist are crucial in developing a sensory diet. Classroom teachers have the responsibility of observation and intervention and of providing reliable feedback to support staff. Creating opportunities for students to move about freely and to have some decision making in determining their sensory levels is essential.

CHAPTER 2

Controversies Concerning Learning Disabilities

Children Are Overdiagnosed with ADHD

Manuel Mota-Castillo

In the following selection psychiatrist Manuel Mota-Castillo describes a case of misdiagnosis of attention deficit hyperactivity disorder (ADHD) that he says is all too commonplace. His patient, a girl he calls Maria, had been diagnosed with ADHD and given the standard treatment of methylphenidate, a kind of amphetamine most commonly sold under the trade name Ritalin. In her case, Mota-Castillo writes, it could not have been more inappropriate, since she was suffering delusions and exhibiting psychotic behavior that put her life in danger. She continued to be misdiagnosed by a variety of health care and social work professionals. Mota-Castillo says this kind of overdiagnosis of ADHD happens in thousands of cases. It results in part, he says, from inadequate guidance in the official manual that professionals use to look up symptoms and their causes, known as the *Diagnostic and Statistical Manual of Mental Disorders,* Fourth Edition, Text Revision. Other factors also lead to overdiagnosis of ADHD, however, and Mota-Castillo lists them and calls for a new approach to classifying the mental illnesses of children.

Photo on previous page. Controversy over the use of ADHD medications such as Adderall is just one of many issues concerning treatment. (Chris Gallagher/Photo Researchers, Inc.)

SOURCE: Manuel Mota-Castillo, "The Crisis of Overdiagnosed ADHD in Children," *Psychiatric Times,* vol. 24, July 1, 2007. Copyright 2007 by CMP Media LLC, 600 Community Drive, Manhasset, NY 11030, USA. Reproduced by permission.

Mota-Castillo is a psychiatrist at the Orlando Regional Behavioral Health Services in Longwood, Florida, and Florida Hospital in Orange City, Florida, as well as medical director of the Grove Academy in Winter Springs, Florida.

This commentary arises from my concern about the superficiality that characterizes the process of diagnosing attention-deficit/hyperactivity disorder (ADHD) in children—usually followed by the prescription of one of the most powerful drugs on earth, methylphenidate. The years pass and I see an even more frightening picture—one in which disorders in children are often given inaccurate and punitive psychiatric diagnoses and treated with inappropriate medication. And yet, the two organizations that represent the majority of American psychiatrists, the American Psychiatric Association (APA) and the American Academy of Child and Adolescent Psychiatry (AACAP) show no sign of worry, despite the terrible consequences that often follow when a disorder is incorrectly diagnosed and treated in emotionally disturbed young people.

Consider the case of María (not her real name), a Hispanic teenager I have been treating for several years. In 2003, María and her mother came to me because the girl had been experiencing hallucinations, racing thoughts, insomnia, elevated mood, and grandiose ideation. She had been taking mixed amphetamine salts prescribed by another psychiatrist who had diagnosed ADHD. No doubt, the psychiatrist had based this diagnosis on features such as increased energy and arousal as well as disruptive behavior and distractibility in the classroom. But the patient's symptoms and family history made me suspicious of a psychotic or affective disorder, especially in light of what María's mother told me: "María is acting exactly like her father, and you know that I have a bad temper and my mother is schizophrenic."

Change of Drug Therapy

I decided to discontinue the mixed amphetamine salts and started giving María quetiapine. Unfortunately, the psychotic process that had been under way for some time could not simply be stopped in its tracks. A week later, the girl's mother called me in desperation because María had just run into oncoming traffic, apparently in response to the ongoing command auditory hallucinations she was experiencing. I advised her mother to take her to the hospital immediately and talked with the doctor on call to discuss my impression that María's symptoms were a common side effect of amphetamines when they are prescribed to individuals with bipolar spectrum disorders.

Despite the obvious red flags for a serious mental illness, María was hospitalized with a primary diagnosis of oppositional defiant disorder (ODD) and ADHD as a secondary diagnosis. In her mental status examination report, the admitting psychiatrist quoted the girl as saying that she was "hearing voices." Yet this doctor wrote, "I am not clear if the patient is really psychotic, or [whether] she is just trying to get what she wants and using the symptoms to her advantage."

> **FAST FACT**
>
> To become a child psychiatrist a person must complete college, followed by four years of medical school, three years of residency training in psychiatry, and two years of specialized training in child psychiatry.

Misdiagnosis Persists

In a discharge summary, the physician noted ADHD as the final diagnosis but sent the girl home on a regimen of 200 mg of quetiapine at bedtime. I suspect this doctor was deferring to my judgment while maintaining his belief that ADHD was the correct diagnosis.

This sort of disposition is all too familiar to me in my practice, which raises the following question: how can competent and caring psychiatrists miss the diagnostic target when assessing patients like María? There may be a few important contributing factors:

- *Failure to obtain a complete family history.* Family history was reported as "negative" by both the in-patient psychiatrist and the outpatient psychiatrist who had preceded me. In reality, the family history was strongly positive, based on my evaluation and treatment of several of the patient's relatives. Specifically, bipolar disorder had been diagnosed in the patient's parents, sister, and maternal cousin; her maternal grandmother had schizophrenia; the paternal grandfather had a history of extreme violence; and her maternal uncle had a history of depression.

- *Cultural and linguistic barriers.* The other doctors involved in María's care did not speak Spanish, and the patient's mother does not speak English. This sort of communication barrier is known to create diagnostic confusion and may interfere with culturally competent treatment.

- *Failure to communicate with clinicians who know the patient well.* Neither the clinician who performed the initial intake nor the evaluating psychiatrist on call that weekend called to speak with me.

- *Misconstruing behaviors as causative explanations.* "Hyperactivity," "oppositional behavior," and "defiance" may be seen in a variety of neuropsychiatric disorders. This does not mean that we should ignore better-defined disorders such as bipolar disorder and reflexively diagnose ADHD or ODD.

María's case illustrates not only the trend toward overdiagnosing ADHD but also the dangers inherent in *DSM*-IV-TR [the *Diagnostic and Statistical Manual of Mental Disorders*, Fourth Edition, Text Revision] diagnoses of conduct disorder and ODD. Both diagnoses may open the door to blaming the victim for behavior that he or she cannot control and denying medical services to patients in desperate need of psychiatric services.

Misreading the Manual

To dissipate any doubt as to how much confusion the ODD diagnosis has brought to the mental health community, suffice it to say that in a note written by the social worker who held a family session with María and her mother, this professional implied that there was a secondary gain in the girl's auditory hallucinations and display of anger, that is, to manipulate her mother. The social worker also noted that the treating psychiatrist labeled María's symptoms as "behavioral" and, therefore, not suitable for inpatient treatment.

Obviously, two experienced professionals forgot that behavior is determined by the patient's psychological functioning (mood, needs, and dynamics). The patient's supposed manipulation of her mother, in my judgment, was an expression of her anger and represented a sign of

Psychiatrists are hampered in diagnosing ADHD because of inadequate diagnosing guidelines in the *Diagnostic and Statistical Manual of Mental Disorders* Fourth Edition, Text Revision. (**Olivier Voisin/ Photo Researchers, Inc.**)

mental illness—not a conscious decision to be bad just for the fun of it. Indeed, the whole concept of the manipulative patient has been carefully deconstructed by [L.] Bowers.

Like the social worker and the psychiatrist in this case, thousands of experienced professionals and psychiatric residents at training centers follow the guidelines set forth in *DSM*-IV-TR. This is why I postulate that a real change in the current child-blaming stance has to start from the top: the APA and the AACAP need to make the first move if we are to influence the writers of the guiding principles in *DSM*-V.

I think that our profession has been in the grips of a kind of post-Freudian denial when it comes to recognizing psychiatric disorders in children. I believe this denial has indirectly contributed to high rates of school dropouts and unnecessary commitments to juvenile detention centers. For example, by the time of her hospitalization, María had already been sent by the school district to a school for the behaviorally disturbed because of her aggression toward teachers and peers as well as her defiance of adult authorities.

Thousands of Cases

In the past 10 years, I have been the medical director at a juvenile detention center and several residential treatment centers. I have reviewed hundreds of cases that started with placement of a youngster in foster care, owing to parental abuse and neglect; and ended up with the child being transferred to a detention facility because of aggressive behavior or sexual acting out, often exacerbated by the ADHD medications wrongly prescribed on the basis of an incorrect diagnosis. . . .

Having seen all too many cases like that of María, I have joined the voices of a few colleagues, such as Charles Huffine and Andres Pumariega, who have called for a more logical approach to diagnosing mental illnesses in

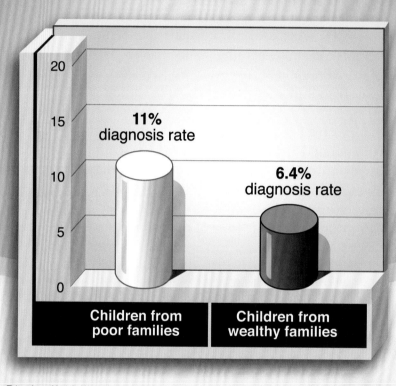

20

15

11%
diagnosis rate

10

6.4%
diagnosis rate

5

0

Children from poor families

Children from wealthy families

Taken from: Mark L. Wolraich, Betsy Busch, and James T. McCracken, "Understanding and Managing the Burden of Pediatric and Adolescent ADHD: Practical Strategies for Diagnosing and Treating ADHD and Comorbidities Across the Continuum of Care," May 5, 2008. http://cme.medscape.com/viewarticle/576428_1.

children. The current *DSM* classification of childhood diseases resembles a collection of recipes in which several "dishes" look very similar, even though they originate from exceedingly different ingredients. That is, *DSM*-IV classification fails to distinguish among conditions presenting with similar symptoms (including, hyperactivity, agitation, increased energy) but arising from vastly different disorders. This problem is exacerbated by diagnostic conclusions based on the clinician's best recollection of *DSM*-IV wording and arrived at after 10- to-15-minute evaluations.

For the sake of children like María, I believe it is time for a change in perspective. We need to open our ears when a mother says, "Doctor, I am bipolar, and I think that my son has what I have."

Children Are Underdiagnosed with ADHD

Steven Reinberg

In the following selection Steven Reinberg reports on a "gold standard" study which concludes that attention deficit hyperactivity disorder (ADHD) is greatly underdiagnosed among children. Indeed, Reinberg reports, the study claims that some 1.2 million children in America have been overlooked. The missed diagnoses are more common among girls than boys, the study finds, and in general children from low-income families are most likely to be underdiagnosed. One doctor that Reinberg interviews claims that ADHD is the most common pyschiatric disorder among children. Reinberg is a health and medical reporter for the HealthDay syndicated news service.

Nearly 9 percent of American children have attention-deficit/hyperactivity disorder (ADHD), but only 32 percent of them are getting the medication they need. That's the sobering conclusion of a landmark new study [2007], the first of its kind based on what doctors consider the "gold standard" of diagnostic criteria—the *Diagnostic and Statistical Manual for Mental Disorders,* Fourth Edition.

"There is a perception that ADHD is overdiagnosed and overtreated," said lead researcher Dr. Tanya E. Froehlich, a developmental-behavioral pediatrician at Cincinnati Children's Medical Center. "But our study shows that for those who meet the criteria for ADHD, the opposite problem—underdiagnosis and undertreatment—seems to be occurring."

Researchers have found that 2.4 million U.S. children aged eight to fifteen have ADHD and estimate that 1.2 million additional children have not been diagnosed or treated. (© Myrleen Pearson/ Alamy)

More than a Million Missed

The researchers found that some 2.4 million children between the ages of 8 and 15 meet the medical definition of ADHD, but an estimated 1.2 million children haven't been diagnosed or treated, Froehlich said, adding that "girls were more likely to be undiagnosed." What's more, children from poor families, who have the highest rates of ADHD, were the least likely to have consistent treatment with medication, Froehlich noted. "In addition, children without health insurance were less likely to be diagnosed and treated," she said. The findings were published in the September issue of *Archives of Pediatrics & Adolescent Medicine*.

ADHD is a condition that becomes apparent in some children in the preschool and early school years and is characterized by hyperactivity, inattention and impulsivity, according to the U.S. National Institute of Mental Health.

FAST FACT

According to the Centers for Disease Control and Prevention, 4.5 million children five to seventeen years of age had been diagnosed with ADHD as of 2006.

National Survey Provides Data

To arrive at their findings, Froehlich and her colleagues collected data on 3,082 children who participated in the National Health and Nutrition Examination Survey. Using interviews, the researchers were able to establish the presence of ADHD. They also used data from doctors and the numbers of ADHD medications being used to establish diagnosis and treatment patterns, according to the report.

The researchers found that of the 8.7 percent of children who met the criteria for ADHD, only 47.9 percent had been diagnosed with the condition and only 32 percent were treated consistently with medications.

Froehlich said medications can be quite effective, and people with ADHD can lead successful lives if they have been properly diagnosed and treated. "There are

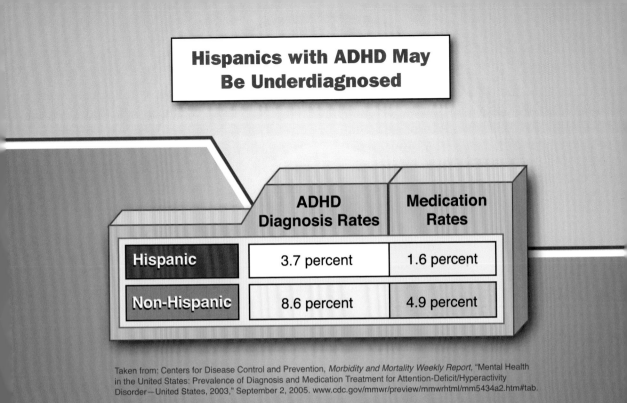

Hispanics with ADHD May Be Underdiagnosed

	ADHD Diagnosis Rates	Medication Rates
Hispanic	3.7 percent	1.6 percent
Non-Hispanic	8.6 percent	4.9 percent

Taken from: Centers for Disease Control and Prevention, *Morbidity and Mortality Weekly Report,* "Mental Health in the United States: Prevalence of Diagnosis and Medication Treatment for Attention-Deficit/Hyperactivity Disorder—United States, 2003," September 2, 2005. www.cdc.gov/mmwr/preview/mmwrhtml/mm5434a2.htm#tab.

many successful professionals who have ADHD," Froehlich said. "On the flip side, there can be a lot of negative consequences associated with the disorder, such as lower rates of school and career achievement and higher rates of substance abuse, incarceration, injuries and car accidents," she said.

Froehlich said more needs to be done to identify and treat children with ADHD. "It's not a trivial disorder," she said. "It can have an impact on the child and the family if it is not diagnosed and addressed. We need to redouble our efforts to help doctors spot the symptoms of ADHD and make an accurate diagnosis."

Poor Children Get Least Care

Dr. Jon A. Shaw, director of child and adolescent psychiatry at the University of Miami School of Medicine, agrees that ADHD is underdiagnosed and undertreated. "The study is confirmatory of the general scientific literature," he said. "ADHD is a highly prevalent disorder, the most common psychiatric diagnosis in children, and that, in general, it is being underdiagnosed and undertreated in our community."

Shaw noted that those children most at risk receive the worst care. "It is clear once again that it is the poorest of our community who are deprived of the benefits of the most effective treatment—psychopharmacology for this condition," he said.

The discovery that ADHD is more common among poorer people is probably related to other risk factors for the disorder, such as use of tobacco, low birth weight and lead exposure, Shaw said.

Medication for ADHD Appears to Improve Brain Function

Lindsey Tanner

Drug treatment for attention deficit hyperactivity disorder is common yet controversial. In the following selection Lindsey Tanner reports on a study that purports to settle the question of whether drug treatment benefits the child or merely pleases teachers and others who prefer a tranquil pupil to a hyperactive one. The study examined the scores of hundreds of children on standardized math and reading tests and found that of the children with ADHD, those who took medication did better on the exams than those who did not. Neither group of ADHD kids did as well as those without the condition, but the study's authors said the benefit of medication was clear. The most common kind of medication for children with ADHD is a stimulant such as Ritalin, which for unknown reasons produces a calming effect on the children. However, the selection notes, only about half of children diagnosed with the disorder receive medication. Tanner is a medical writer for the Associated Press.

SOURCE: Lindsey Tanner, "Study Links ADHD Medicine with Better Test Scores," Associated Press, April 27, 2009. Reprinted with permission of the Associated Press.

Children on medicine for attention deficit disorder scored higher on academic tests than their unmedicated peers in the first large, long-term study suggesting this kind of benefit from the widely used drugs.

The nationally representative study involved nearly 600 children with attention deficit hyperactivity disorder followed from kindergarten through fifth grade.

Children's scores on several standardized math and reading tests taken during those years were examined. Compared with unmedicated kids, average scores for medicated children were almost three points higher in math and more than five points higher in reading. The difference amounts to about three months ahead in reading and two months in math, the researchers said.

Both groups had lower scores on average than a separate group of children without ADHD. The researchers acknowledged that gap but said the benefits for medicated youngsters were still notable.

"We're not trying to say in this study that medication is the only answer," but the results suggest benefits that parents, educators and policy-makers shouldn't ignore, said Richard Scheffler, the lead author and professor at the University of California at Berkeley's School of Public Health.

The researchers agreed that other treatment ADHD children often receive—including behavior therapy and tutoring—can help, but the study didn't look at those measures.

Most ADHD drug users in the study were on stimulants; the study didn't identify which ones.

About 4 million U.S. children have been diagnosed with ADHD. About half of them take prescription medication—often powerful stimulants like Ritalin—to control the extreme fidgetiness and impulsive behavior that characterize the condition.

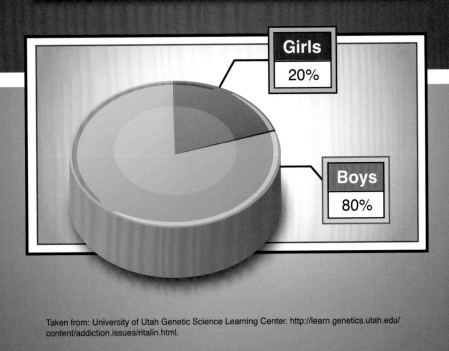

Ritalin Is Currently Prescribed to Approximately 4.5 Million U.S. Children

Girls
20%

Boys
80%

Taken from: University of Utah Genetic Science Learning Center. http://learn.genetics.utah.edu/content/addiction.issues/ritalin.html.

Often, kids with ADHD struggle in class and get lower grades than their classmates. They also have higher dropout rates.

American Academy of Pediatrics guidelines say stimulant drugs are effective but that behavior techniques should also be used.

Teachers often advocate medication because it can calm disruptive behavior. But it's a contentious issue for many parents, worried about putting their kids on drugs that can have side-effects including decreased appetite, weight loss and insomnia.

Previous evidence suggests teachers give higher grades to ADHD kids on medication, but the study authors said that might simply mean teachers prefer them because they're better behaved than unmedicated children.

Proponents of ADHD medication point out that Ritalin produces a calming affect on children that allows them to focus on tasks more easily. (© Catchlight Visual Services/Alamy)

They said theirs is the largest, longest-duration study based on objective standardized academic tests suggesting that medicated kids may be better learners, too.

Psychiatrist Dr. Bennett Leventhal, who was not involved in the study, called the results impressive.

"It doesn't mean that every child with ADHD should be taking medication," but previous studies have suggested that most affected kids can benefit, said Leventhal, a University of Illinois–Chicago psychiatry professor.

The study appears in the May issue of *Pediatrics*, released Monday. A federal grant paid for the research; the authors said they have no financial ties to ADHD drug-makers.

Dr. Louis Kraus, a psychiatrist with Chicago's Rush University Medical Center, said he worries the study will make parents turn to medication without considering other options. Behavioral treatment generally should be tried first, Kraus said.

Blake Taylor, a 19-year-old Berkeley sopho-more who's been on ADHD medication since age 5, said the results aren't surprising.

Medication "doesn't make me smarter," he said, "it allows me to focus, to be more orga-nized."

He recalled doing poorly on a high school exam that he'd studied hard for, but he hadn't taken his ADHD medication that day. He said his mind kept wandering, thinking about war posters on the classroom walls and noise from children playing outside.

Taylor said when he was younger he some-times skipped his medicine because, like many teens, "I didn't want to be different from my other class-mates." Taking his medication was a reminder, he said.

His other treatments have included counseling and organizational tutoring; Taylor said daily cardio and weightlifting workouts help, too, using up excess energy.

> **FAST FACT**
>
> Studies indicate that when taken as pre-scribed, in slow-acting pill form, Ritalin is not addictive. However, if crushed and injected, the medication can lead to addiction and other dangerous side effects.

Medication for ADHD May Harm Brain Function

Edmund S. Higgins

Stimulant drugs are widely prescribed for children with attention deficit hyperactivity disorder. In the following selection Edmund S. Higgins, an expert in the field of child psychiatry and drug therapies, describes concerns about possible detrimental effects of long-term use. He agrees that several studies have established the benefits of Ritalin and similar stimulant drugs, and that studies have discredited some claimed risks. However, Higgins remains concerned that the drugs may elevate anxiety, foster addiction, and even cause hallucinations over the long term. He counsels more caution in prescribing stimulants and encourages the exploration of alternatives such as brain training.

Higgins is a clinical associate professor of family medicine and psychiatry at the Medical University of South Carolina and the coauthor of several relevant books.

A few years ago a single mother who had recently moved to town came to my office asking me to prescribe the stimulant drug Adderall for her sixth-grade son. The boy had been taking the medication for several years, and his mother had liked its effects:

SOURCE: Edmund S. Higgins, "Do ADHD Drugs Take a Toll on the Brain?" *Scientific American Mind*, vol. 20, 2009, pp. 38–43. Copyright © 2009 by Scientific American, a division of Nature America, Inc. All rights reserved. Reprinted with permission. www.sciam.com.

it made homework time easier and improved her son's grades.

At the time of this visit, the boy was off the medication, and I conducted a series of cognitive and behavioral tests on him. He performed wonderfully. I also noticed that off the medication he was friendly and playful. On a previous casual encounter, when the boy had been on Adderall, he had seemed reserved and quiet. His mother acknowledged this was a side effect of the Adderall. I told her that I did not think her son had attention-deficit hyperactivity disorder (ADHD) and that he did not need medication. That was the last time I saw her.

Attention-deficit hyperactivity disorder afflicts about 5 percent of U.S. children—twice as many boys as girls—age six to 17, according to a recent survey conducted by the Centers for Disease Control and Prevention. As its name implies, people with the condition have trouble focusing and often are hyperactive or impulsive. An estimated 9 percent of boys and 4 percent of girls in the U.S. are taking stimulant medications as part of their therapy for ADHD, the CDC reported in 2005. The majority of patients take methylphenidate (Ritalin, Concerta), whereas most of the rest are prescribed an amphetamine such as Adderall.

Although it sounds counterintuitive to give stimulants to a person who is hyperactive, these drugs are thought to boost activity in the parts of the brain responsible for attention and self-control. Indeed, the pills can improve attention, concentration and productivity and also suppress impulsive behavior, producing significant improvements in some people's lives. Severe inattention and impulsivity put individuals at risk for substance abuse, unemployment, crime and car accidents. Thus, appropriate medication might keep a person out of prison, away from addictive drugs or in a job.

Over the past 15 years, however, doctors have been pinning the ADHD label on—and prescribing stimulants for—a rapidly rising number of patients, including those with moderate to mild inattention, some of whom, like the sixth grader I saw, have a normal ability to focus. This trend may be fueled in part by a relaxation of official diagnostic criteria for the disorder, combined with a lower tolerance in society for mild behavioral or cognitive problems.

In addition, patients are no longer just taking the medicines for a few years during grade school but are encouraged to stay on them into adulthood. In 2008 two new stimulants—Vyvanse (amphetamine) and Concerta—received U.S. Food and Drug Administration indications for treating adults, and pharmaceutical firms are pushing awareness of the adult forms of the disorder. What is more, many people who have no cognitive deficits are opting to take these drugs to boost their academic performance. A number of my patients—doctors, lawyers and other professionals—have asked me for stimulants in hopes of boosting their productivity. As a result of these developments, prescriptions for methylphenidate and amphetamine rose by almost 12 percent a year between 2000 and 2005, according to a 2007 study.

With the expanded and extended use of stimulants comes mounting concern that the drugs might take a toll on the brain over the long run. Indeed, a smattering of recent studies, most of them involving animals, hint that stimulants could alter the structure and function of the brain in ways that may depress mood, boost anxiety and, contrary to their short-term effects, lead to cognitive deficits. Human studies already indicate the medications can adversely affect areas of the brain that govern growth in children, and some researchers worry that additional harms have yet to be unearthed.

Medicine for the Mind

To appreciate why stimulants could have negative effects over time, it helps to first understand what they do in the

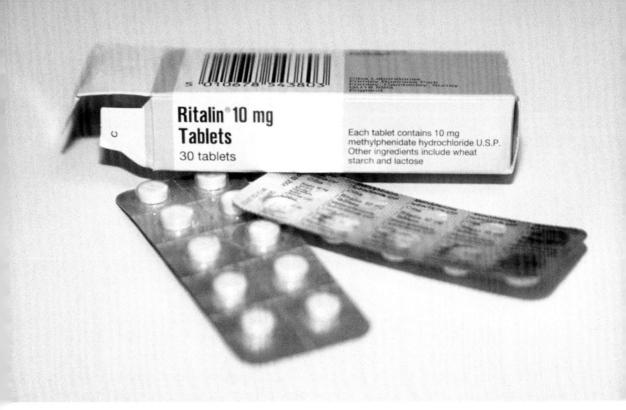

Ritalin® 10 mg
Tablets
30 tablets

Each tablet contains 10 mg
methylphenidate hydrochloride U.S.P.
Other ingredients include wheat
starch and lactose

brain. One hallmark of ADHD is an underactive frontal cortex, a brain region that lies just behind the forehead and controls such "executive" functions as decision making, predicting future events, and suppressing emotions and urges. This area may, in some cases, be smaller than average in ADHD patients, compromising their executive abilities. Frontal cortex function depends greatly on a signaling chemical, or neurotransmitter, called dopamine, which is released in this structure by neurons that originate in deeper brain structures. Less dopamine in the prefrontal cortex is linked, for example, with cognitive difficulty in old age. Another set of dopamine-releasing neurons extends to the nucleus accumbens, a critical mediator of motivation, pleasure and reward whose function may also be impaired in ADHD.

Stimulants enhance communication in these dopamine-controlled brain circuits by binding to so-called dopamine transporters—the proteins on nerve endings that suck up excess dopamine—thereby deactivating them.

With the increased use of stimulants such as Ritalin come concerns that, with extended use, such drugs may have a detrimental effect on the brain. (Tracy Dominey/Photo Researchers, Inc.)

As a result, dopamine accumulates outside the neurons, and the additional neurotransmitter is thought to improve the operation of neuronal circuits critical for motivation and impulse control.

Not only can methylphenidate and amphetamine ameliorate a mental deficit, they also can enhance cognitive performance. In studies dating back to the 1970s, researchers have shown that normal children who do not have ADHD also become more attentive—and often calmer—after taking stimulants. In fact, the drugs can lead to higher test scores in students of average and above-average intellectual ability.

Since the 1950s, when doctors first started prescribing stimulants to treat behavior problems, millions of people have taken them without obvious incident. A number of studies have even exonerated them from causing possible adverse effects. For example, researchers have failed to find differences between stimulant-treated children and those not on meds in the larger-scale growth of the brain. In January 2009 child psychiatrist Philip Shaw of the National Institute of Mental Health and his colleagues used MRI scans to measure the change in the thickness of the cerebral cortex (the outer covering of the brain) of 43 youths between the ages of 12 and 16 who had ADHD. The researchers found no evidence that stimulants slowed cortical growth. In fact, only the unmedicated adolescents showed more thinning of the cerebrum than was typical for their age, hinting that the drugs might facilitate normal cortical development in kids with ADHD.

Altering Mood

Despite such positive reports, traces of a sinister side to stimulants have also surfaced. In February 2007 the FDA issued warnings about side effects such as growth stunting and psychosis, among other mental disorders. Indeed, the vast majority of adults with ADHD experience

Most Common Adverse Side Effects of Ritalin

Most commonly reported adverse effects in people taking methylphenidate:

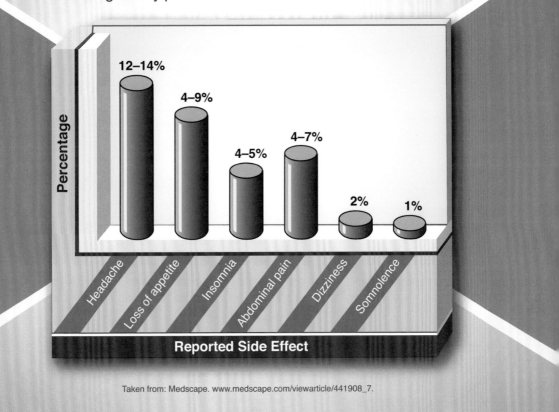

Taken from: Medscape. www.medscape.com/viewarticle/441908_7.

at least one additional psychiatric illness—often an anxiety disorder or drug addiction—in their lifetime. Having ADHD is itself a risk factor for other mental health problems, but the possibility also exists that stimulant treatment during childhood might contribute to these high rates of accompanying diagnoses.

After all, stimulants activate the brain's reward pathways, which are part of the neural circuitry that controls mood under normal conditions. And at least three studies using animals hint that exposure to methylphenidate during childhood may alter mood in the long run, perhaps raising the risk of depression and anxiety in adulthood.

In an experiment published in 2003 psychiatrist Eric Nestler of the University of Texas Southwestern Medical Center and his colleagues injected juvenile rats twice a day with a low dose of methylphenidate similar to that prescribed for children with ADHD. When the rats became adults, the scientists observed the rodents' responses to various emotional stimuli. The rodents that had received methylphenidate were significantly less responsive to natural rewards such as sugar, sex, and fun, novel environments than were untreated rats, suggesting that the drug-exposed animals find such stimuli less pleasurable. In addition, the stimulants apparently made the rats more sensitive to stressful situations such as being forced to swim inside a large tube. Similarly, in the same year psychiatrist William Carlezon of Harvard Medical School and his colleagues reported that methylphenidate-treated preadolescent rats displayed a muted response to a cocaine reward as adults as well as unusual apathy in a forced-swim test, a sign of depression.

> **FAST FACT**
>
> A controversial study published in the *American Journal of Psychiatry* in 2009 claims that stimulants prescribed for the treatment of ADHD raise the risk of cardiac arrest in children and teens.

In 2008 psychopharmacologist Leandro F. Vendruscolo and his co-workers at Federal University of Santa Catarina in Brazil echoed these results using spontaneously hypertensive rats, which—like children with ADHD—sometimes show attention deficits, hyperactivity and motor impulsiveness. The researchers injected these young rats with methylphenidate for 16 days at doses approximating those used to treat ADHD in young people. Four weeks later, when the rats were young adults, those that had been exposed to methylphenidate were unusually anxious: they avoided traversing the central area of an open, novel space more so than did rats not exposed to methylphenidate. Adverse effects of this stimulant, the authors speculate, could contribute to the high rates of anxiety disorders among ADHD patients.

Copying Cocaine?

The long-term use of any drug that affects the brain's reward circuitry also raises the specter of addiction. Methylphenidate has a chemical structure similar to that of cocaine and acts on the brain in a very similar way. Both cocaine and methamphetamine (also called "speed" or "meth")—another highly addictive stimulant—block dopamine transporters just as ADHD drugs do. In the case of the illicit drugs, the dopamine surge is so sudden that in addition to making a person unusually energetic and alert, it produces a "high."

Recent experiments in animals have sounded the alarm that methylphenidate may alter the brain in ways similar to that of more powerfully addictive stimulants such as cocaine. In February 2009 neuroscientists Yong Kim and Paul Greengard, along with their colleagues at the Rockefeller University, reported cocainelike structural and chemical alterations in the brains of mice given methylphenidate. The researchers injected the mice with either methylphenidate or cocaine daily for two weeks. Both treatments increased the density of tiny extensions called spines at the ends of neurons bearing dopamine receptors in the rodent nucleus accumbens. Compared with cocaine, methylphenidate had a somewhat more localized influence; it also had more power over longer spines and less effect on shorter ones. Otherwise, the drugs' effects were strikingly similar.

Furthermore, the scientists found that methylphenidate boosted the amount of a protein called FosB, which turns genes on and off, even more than cocaine did. That result could be a chemical warning of future problems: excess FosB heightens an animal's sensitivity to the rewarding effects of cocaine and makes the animal more likely to ingest the drug. Many former cocaine addicts struggle with depression, anxiety and cognitive problems. Researchers have found that cocaine has remodeled the brains of such ex-users. Similar problems—principally, perhaps, difficulty experiencing joy and excitement in life—could occur after many years of Ritalin or Adderall use.

Amphetamine and methylphenidate can also be addictive if abused by, say, crushing or snorting the pills. In a classic study published in 1995 research psychiatrist Nora Volkow, then at Stony Brook University, and her colleagues showed that injections of methylphenidate produced a cocainelike high in volunteers. More than seven million people in the U.S. have abused methylphenidate, and as many as 750,000 teenagers and young adults show signs of addiction, according to a 2006 report.

Typical oral doses of ADHD meds rarely produce such euphoria and are not usually addicting. Furthermore, the evidence to date, including two 2008 studies from the National Institute on Drug Abuse, indicates that children treated with stimulants early in life are not more likely than other children to become addicted to drugs as adults. In fact, the risk for severe cases of ADHD may run in the opposite direction. (A low addiction risk also jibes with Carlezon's earlier findings, which indicated that methylphenidate use in early life mutes adult rats' response to cocaine.)

Corrupting Cognition

Amphetamines such as Adderall could alter the mind in other ways. A team led by psychologist Stacy A. Castner of the Yale University School of Medicine has documented long-lasting behavioral oddities, such as hallucinations, and cognitive impairment in rhesus monkeys that received escalating injected doses of amphetamine over either six or 12 weeks. Compared with monkeys given inactive saline, the drug-treated monkeys displayed deficits in working memory—the short-term buffer that allows us to hold several items in mind—which persisted for at least three years after exposure to the drug. The researchers connected these cognitive problems to a significantly lower level of dopamine activity in the frontal cortex of the drug-treated monkeys as compared with that of the monkeys not given amphetamine.

Underlying such cognitive and behavioral effects may be subtle structural changes too small to show up on brain scans. In a 1997 study psychologists Terry E. Robinson and Bryan Kolb of the University of Michigan at Ann Arbor found that high injected doses of amphetamine in rats cause the major output neurons of the nucleus accumbens to sprout longer branches, or dendrites, as well as additional spines on those dendrites. A decade later Castner's team linked lower doses of amphetamine to subtle atrophy of neurons in the prefrontal cortex of monkeys.

A report published in 2005 by neurologist George A. Ricaurte and his team at the Johns Hopkins University School of Medicine is even more damning to ADHD meds because the researchers used realistic doses and drug delivery by mouth instead of by injection. Ricaurte's group trained baboons and squirrel monkeys to self-administer an oral formulation of amphetamine similar to Adderall: the animals drank an amphetamine-laced orange cocktail twice a day for four weeks, mimicking the dosing schedule in humans. Two to four weeks later the researchers detected evidence of amphetamine-induced brain damage, encountering lower levels of dopamine and fewer dopamine transporters on nerve endings in the striatum—a trio of brain regions that includes the nucleus accumbens—in amphetamine-treated primates than in untreated animals. The authors believe these observations reflect a drug-related loss of dopamine-releasing nerve fibers that reach the striatum from the brain stem.

One possible consequence of a loss of dopamine and its associated molecules is Parkinson's disease, a movement disorder that can also lead to cognitive deficits. A study in humans published in 2006 hints at a link between Parkinson's and a prolonged exposure to amphetamine in any form (not just that prescribed for ADHD). Before Parkinson's symptoms such as tremors and muscle rigidity appear, however, dopamine's function in the brain must decline by 80 to 90 percent, or by about twice as much as what Ricaurte and his colleagues saw in baboons that were drinking a more moderate dose of the drug. And some studies have found no connection between stimulant use and Parkinson's.

Stimulants do seem to stunt growth in children. Otherwise, however, studies in humans have largely failed to demonstrate any clear indications of harm from taking ADHD medications as prescribed. Whether the drugs alter the human brain in the same way they alter that of certain animals is unknown, because so far little clinical data exist on their long-term neurological effects. Even when the dosing is similar or the animals have something resembling ADHD, different species' brains may have varying sensitivities to stimulant medications.

Nevertheless, in light of the emerging evidence, many doctors and researchers are recommending a more cautious approach to the medical use of stimulants. Some are urging the adoption of strict diagnostic criteria for ADHD and a policy restricting prescriptions for individuals who fit those criteria. Others are advocating behavior modification—which can be as effective as stimulants over the long run—as a first-line approach to combating the disorder. Certain types of mental exercises may also ease ADHD symptoms. For patients who require stimulants, some neurologists and psychiatrists have also suggested using the lowest dose needed or monitoring the blood levels of these drugs as a way of keeping concentrations below those shown to be problematic in other mammals. Without these or similar measures, large numbers of people who regularly take stimulants may ultimately struggle with a new set of problems spawned by the treatments themselves.

Most Kids with Autism Are Not Mentally Retarded

Meredyth Goldberg Edelson

In the following selection psychologist Meredyth Goldberg Edelson systematically examines the claim that the majority of children with autism also suffer from mental retardation. She notes that there was a two-decade gap between the first diagnosis of autism and the first claim that the condition overlaps with mental retardation in most cases. She traces that claim to a 1961 paper by researcher Mildred Creak, who, she says, did not offer any evidence for the assertion that mental retardation frequently accompanies autism. In the years since, Edelson says, it has become commonplace to report that anywhere from two-thirds to nine out of ten autistic children are retarded. However, Edelson's review of the literature finds insufficient evidence to uphold these claims. She argues that the most reliable studies point to a rate of between 40 and 54 percent.

Edelson is a professor of psychology at Willamette University in Salem, Oregon. She has a research interest in autism and other behavior disorders in children.

SOURCE: Meredyth Goldberg Edelson, "Are the Majority of Children with Autism Mentally Retarded? A Systematic Evaluation of the Data," *Focus on Autism and Other Developmental Disabilities,* Summer 2006, p. 66. Reproduced by permission.

Autism was first described by [physician Leo] Kanner, who maintained that children with autism had normal intellectual functioning; he stated that "even though most of these children were at one time or another looked upon as feebleminded, they are all unquestionably endowed with good *cognitive potentialities*." Kanner never systematically nor empirically assessed the intelligence of individuals with autism; his statements were made based on observations of 11 children. There were, however, early studies that did obtain empirical evidence regarding the intelligence of children with autism; rates of MR [mental retardation] in samples of children with autism were typically between 30% and 40% in these reports, much lower than the rates cited today. Questions arise as to when the assumptions about the rates of MR in children with autism changed and, more importantly, upon what evidence they changed.

[Researcher Mildred] Creak was the first author to make a claim that children with autism were likely to have MR. As part of a working group for establishing diagnostic criteria for autism in Great Britain, Creak described nine criteria for schizophrenic syndrome of childhood, one of which was "a background of serious retardation in which islets of normal, near normal, or exceptional functioning or skill may appear." In a subsequent paper, Creak again claimed that the psychotic child "is the most ineducable of any." The empirical evidence at the time, while scant, did not support Creak's assertions that there was *generally* a "background of serious retardation," and Creak herself never cited any evidence for her claims. However, shortly after Creak's publications, researchers began finding much higher rates of MR in children with autism, and this seemed to follow other nonempirical claims that could be traced back to Creak. Since then, hundreds of additional claims have been made, and currently it is commonly reported that between 67% and 90% of children with autism also have MR.

Claims Need to Be Examined

To date, no systematic examination of the evidence for the claims regarding the rates of MR in children with autism has been conducted. In view of this, the purpose of the present study was to examine the origin of the statistics regarding the high prevalence rates of MR in children with autism to ascertain the nature of the support for these statistics. Before this examination can take place, it is important first to understand how a diagnosis of MR

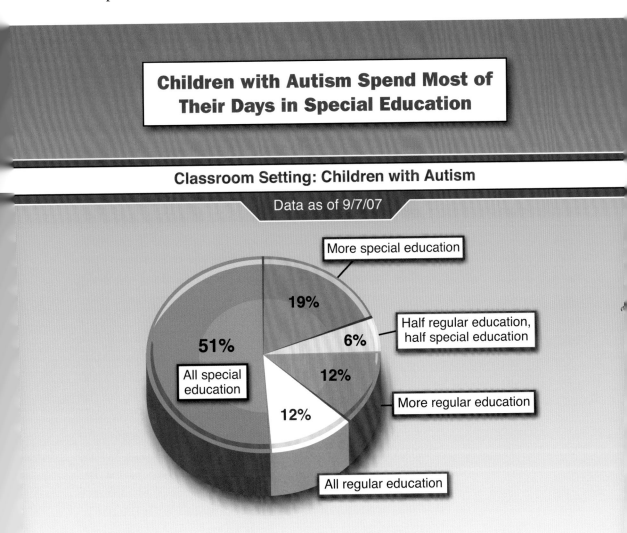

Children with Autism Spend Most of Their Days in Special Education

Classroom Setting: Children with Autism

Data as of 9/7/07

- More special education — 19%
- Half regular education, half special education — 6%
- More regular education — 12%
- All regular education — 12%
- All special education — 51%

Taken from: Interactive Autism Network. www.iancommunity.org/galleries/report3-gallery/Classroom_Setting_Autism.jpg.

is made and how intelligence level is typically assessed. A diagnosis of MR is based on three criteria: cognitive impairments defined by IQ scores less than 70, adaptive skills deficits, and age of onset prior to 18 years. . . .

Most Studies Are Flawed

Seventy-four percent of the claims about the prevalence of MR in individuals with autism came from nonempirical articles; 26% derived from empirical studies. Of the nonempirical articles, 36% never provided a citation in support of the claim. Of the 106 nonempirical articles that did make citations, 8% of the citations failed to provide supporting evidence for the claim, and 21% reported higher prevalence rates than those reported in the articles that the authors cited. Finally, of the 165 nonempirical articles that made claims about the prevalence of MR in individuals with autism, 88 (53%) of the citations never traced back to empirical data when the reference trail was followed historically. . . .

FAST FACT

A 2006 study of children with autism in seven states found those with mental retardation (indicated by an IQ of 70 or less) ranged from 33 to 59 percent.

Link to Retardation Unproven

In view of the present findings on these three issues, the conclusion that the majority of children with autism also have MR does not seem warranted. Most of the claims originate from nonempirical sources that (a) do not trace to empirical data, (b) cite empirical research that is 25 to 45 years old, (c) used inappropriate measures, or (d) typically failed to acknowledge the possible interference of autism on the assessment of intelligence. Furthermore, only 15.7% of all claims made actually traced to empirical data that were obtained from studies whose authors described specific methods used to assess intelligence. Thus, only a small percentage of studies reported methods that could be evaluated with regard to their validity.

Although recent data have shown that some children with autism do, in fact, have MR, the rates are much lower than the high prevalence rates cited in the past. Recent epidemiological surveys have shown that the prevalence rates of MR in children with autism is between 40% and 55%, much lower than the typical rates cited in the literature. Recent empirical studies indicate that when appropriate measures of intelligence are used—those that take into account the interference of autism—a significantly lower prevalence rate of MR is found relative to the rates typically reported in the literature. However, the practice of claiming that a majority of children with autism are mentally retarded continues largely unabated. . . .

Given the present results, it seems prudent to obtain additional empirical evidence before making any definitive conclusions regarding the prevalence rates of MR in children with autism. Empirical studies need

Earlier research claiming that most autistic children also have mental retardation (MR) was flawed, the author contends, pointing to new findings showing that MR rates are actually much lower than those previously cited. (**Burger/Phanie/ Photo Researchers, Inc.**)

to be conducted in which measures of intelligence take into account the interfering symptoms of autism on the process of assessment, examiners are knowledgeable about and have experience in assessing children with autism, and modifications to the testing situation are made to minimize the "construct-irrelevant" error in test outcome. Until that time, researchers in the autism field should use caution when making assumptions or citing claims about the rates of MR in children with autism.

Autism Is Linked to Mental Retardation Through Genetic Syndrome

Jamie Newton

Autism is a condition that renders children unable to interact with others in a socially normal way, and sometimes renders them unable to speak or learn. In the following selection Jamie Newton reports on research that may have uncovered a link to genes that are known to cause mental retardation, which sometimes but certainly not always accompanies autism. The genes are responsible for a disorder called tuberous sclerosis complex, or TSC, that leads to lesions in the brain and elsewhere. The researchers discovered that the same malfunctioning genes may be responsible for faulty wiring in the brain. When the genes are not working properly, brain cells called neurons grow too many connections with other neurons, disrupting the normal flow of signals. The researchers believe they may have found a link to autism in this condition, which occurs in about half of autism patients. They are hopeful that they can develop genetic therapy to address it. Newton is the director of media relations at Children's Hospital Boston.

SOURCE: Children's Hospital Boston, "News Release: Rare Genetic Disorder Gives Clues to Autism, Epilepsy, Mental Retardation," September 23, 2008. Reproduced by permission.

Arare genetic disorder called tuberous sclerosis complex (TSC) is yielding insight into a possible cause of some neurodevelopmental disorders: structural abnormalities in neurons, or brain cells. Researchers in the F.M. Kirby Neurobiology Center at Children's Hospital Boston, led by Mustafa Sahin, MD, PhD, and Xi He, PhD, also found that normal neuronal structure can potentially be restored.

If this could be done safely in humans, it might be possible to ameliorate the symptoms of epilepsy, mental retardation and autism, which are frequent complications of TSC, say the researchers. Their findings, accompanied by commentary, were the cover article of the September 15 [2008] issue of *Genes & Development*.

FAST FACT

As the characterization of the autism "spectrum" has broadened, the percentage of diagnosed children who are also mentally retarded has gone down from as many as 80 percent to as few as 26 percent.

Lesions Lead to Trouble

TSC causes benign tumor-like lesions, which can affect every organ in the body and are called tubers when they occur in the brain. In the study, Sahin, He, lead author Yong-Jin Choi, PhD, and colleagues show in mice that when the two genes linked to the disease, TSC1 and TSC2, are inactivated, neurons grow too many axons (the long nerve fibers that transmit signals). Normal neurons grow just one axon and multiple dendrites (short projections that receive input from other neurons). This specification of axons and dendrites, known as polarity, is crucial for proper information flow.

"We think if initial polarity is not formed properly, the result will be abnormal connectivity in the brain," says Sahin, who also directs the clinical Multi-Disciplinary Tuberous Sclerosis Program at Children's.

Autism Link Suspected

Since autism occurs in about half of people with TSC, the findings support the idea that such miswiring causes

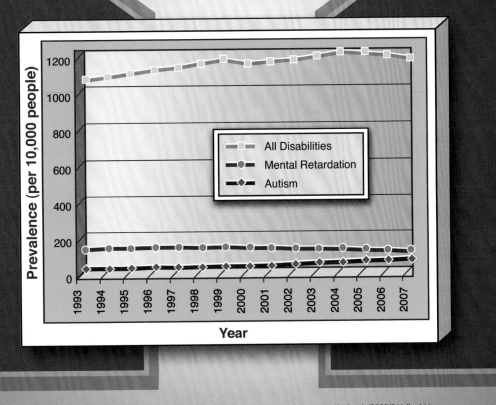

The Incidence of Retardation Exceeds That of Autism, but the Gap Is Shrinking

Prevalence of Autism, Mental Retardation, and All Disabilities

Taken from: A Photon in the Darkness. http://photoninthedarkness.com/wp-content/uploads/2009/01/all_cht.jpg.
Data taken from the U.S. Department of Education.

or contributes to autism, Sahin adds. He has received funding from Autism Speaks, the Manton Foundation and the Tuberous Sclerosis Alliance to pursue this idea further.

"People have started to look at autism as a developmental disconnection syndrome—there are either too many connections or too few connections between different parts of the brain," Sahin says. "In mouse models of TSC, we're seeing an exuberance of connections."

In laboratory experiments, the researchers were able to limit multiple axon formation by using the cancer drug rapamycin to suppress production of a protein called SAD-A kinase. This protein is produced in excess when the TSC1 and TSC2 genes are inactivated, and is found in abundance in the abnormally large cells that make up tubers.

Hope for Therapy

Because increased SAD-A is associated with increased axon growth, the researchers also speculate that the TSC pathway could be manipulated to regenerate or repair

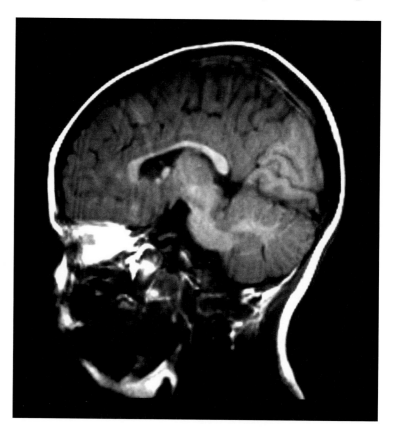

A brain scan shows the lesions (white area) typical of tuberous sclerosis complex (TSC). Because half of people with TSC also have autism, scientists suspect the two conditions are linked. (Living Art Enterprises, LLC/Photo Researchers, Inc.)

axons lost or damaged in spinal cord or other nerve injuries. "These findings provide a potential explanation for neurological abnormalities in TSC patients and perhaps in people without TSC," says He. "The challenge remains as to how to treat these conditions. We have some clues but a lot more research needs to be done."

The study was funded by grants from the Tuberous Sclerosis Alliance, the Manton Foundation, the Hearst Fund and the National Institutes of Health.

Traumatic Experiences Can Give Rise to Learning Disability Symptoms

Claudia Meininger Gold

The symptoms of attention deficit hyperactivity disorder do not always indicate that the condition is present. Other causes may lead to the same behavior. In the following selection pediatrician Claudia Meininger Gold describes how a child's unresolved grief can produce the very symptoms of ADHD and how this all too often leads to inappropriate and ineffective medication. The child she treated was just five years old when her teacher referred her for evaluation of potential ADHD with a request that medication be prescribed. The teacher was concerned because the girl had been disruptive in class, but when Gold talked with the parents she learned some surprising facts that indicated something other than ADHD was going on. What the girl actually needed was not medication but grief therapy. According to Gold, many grieving children receive ADHD medication inappropriately. She calls for more effort to invest the time and human effort to help such children rather than race to write a prescription.

Gold practices behavioral pediatrics at Macony Pediatric & Adolescent Medicine P.C. in Great Barrington, Massachusetts.

SOURCE: Claudia Meininger Gold, "Medicating Your Grief Won't Help You Heal," *Boston Globe*, April 27, 2009. Reproduced by permission of the author.

On a recent [2009] episode of the HBO series *In Treatment*, a CEO [chief executive officer] of a major company describes with complete absence of emotion the death of his 16-year-old brother when he was 6. When Paul, his therapist, suggests that his panic attacks may be related, he leaves the office, saying he will ask his doctor to prescribe medication now that he has a diagnosis. Paul gently suggests that they continue the important work they have begun. I am eager to see how this plays out. I am quite certain, however, that in the real world, the CEO would find many doctors to prescribe medication, enabling him to eliminate the symptom without the hard work of grieving.

This episode reminded me of a case in my pediatric practice (with the details changed to protect privacy). A 5-year-old girl was referred by her kindergarten teacher for evaluation of attention deficit hyperactivity disorder, with a strong recommendation that medication be considered. Her behavior had been disruptive since preschool, but was now affecting her ability to learn. There was concern that she might not be able to move on to first grade. Before I even saw the patient, armed with standardized forms and psychological testing, I was quite sure that she would meet diagnostic criteria for ADHD and that medication would be a reasonable consideration.

An Underlying Issue

I met with her parents, who described classic symptoms of ADHD, including prolonged battles at home around such simple tasks as getting dressed for school. About halfway through the visit, I began to ask, as I always do, about past history. "How was your pregnancy with her?" There was a pause, during which the parents exchanged looks. "Actually, I'm not her biological mother."

Now it was my turn to pause, as I was quite shocked to receive this important piece of information so late in

Sometimes a child's grief can be erroneously diagnosed as ADHD. (© Catchlight Visual Services/Alamy)

the evaluation process. With some reluctance, they went on to tell me that the girl's mother was seriously mentally ill, had been intermittently involved in her life, and had disappeared completely two years earlier. But, they assured me, she never talked about her mother and it wasn't an important issue.

This story has a happy ending. I agreed that medication could be helpful, but, building on the trust they had developed with me as their pediatrician, I suggested that the loss of her mother was actually very important and needed to be addressed. They accepted my referral to a therapist. I am fortunate to have an excellent colleague across the street who accepts their insurance. He wisely explained to them that children do grieve, and now the whole family is engaged in working with him around this painful and difficult task. This child is now thriving in first grade.

The Overmedication of Grief

For this one positive outcome, there are hundreds that do not end this way. Children who have experienced terrible loss do not have the opportunity this girl had. They are aggressive and disruptive, and their symptoms are medicated away. They continue to struggle, often failing in school. Some of the reasons this path is chosen are lack of time, limited access to mental health services, and resistance to doing this hard work.

I recently received a letter from the state with the alarming statistic that 37 percent (nearly $190 million) of the MassHealth pharmacy budget is spent on behavioral health medication. The letter asks for input regarding possible ways to improve patient care while reducing costs.

I proposed that we as a society recognize that grief and loss cannot be medicated away. As one friend who recently lost her husband so eloquently put it, "Grief is a powerful release that validates your loss, relieves stress, and helps you heal." Certainly medication may be an adjunct, particularly when people are so incapacitated by their symptoms that they are unable to function. But if we as a culture

> **FAST FACT**
>
> According to Hospice Net, many pediatric psychiatrists say that it is normal for a child who has just lost a parent or loved one to engage in denial and claim that the family member is still alive.

validate the experience of grief, if we offer the time and space and resources to support people through the difficult process, I am quite certain that in the long run we will not only spend less on medication, but will help people to heal and return to being productive members of society. It is with children that this investment will have the greatest return.

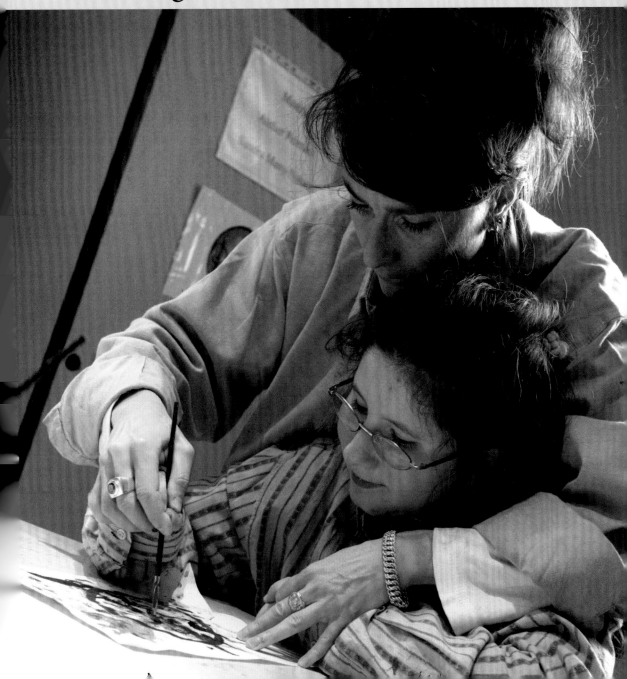

CHAPTER **3**

Personal Experiences with Learning Disabilities

A Mother Finds That Technology Helps Her Dyslexic Daughter Succeed

Jacqueline L. Salmon

Jacqueline L. Salmon remembers exactly when her attempts to help her daughter Sarah cope with dyslexia hit bottom. In the following selection she recounts the painful scene as a turning point toward a better time. Sarah always liked books but always trailed behind other children in her reading ability, Salmon recalls. She was eventually diagnosed with dyslexia. But even then her parents struggled to find a way to help Sarah read better. At last, they discovered that technology could help. Recorded books, intended for the blind, were a boon to Sarah, Salmon writes. Other kinds of computer-based assistive technology has also proved valuable. Once Sarah was able to move from the written word to oral learning, her achievement level rose spectacularly. Salmon is a staff journalist with the *Washington Post*. She has also written for other publications, including the *Los Angeles Times*.

Photo on previous page. People who have learning disabilities need special education to help them develop social and learning skills. **(Burger/Phanie/ Photo Researchers, Inc.)**

SOURCE: Jacqueline L. Salmon, "Reading, Writing & Frustration," *Washington Post Magazine*, April 15, 2007, p. W18. Copyright © 2007, the Washington Post. Reprinted with permission.

The turning point in the struggle with our daughter's dyslexia came during Sarah's sophomore year in high school. She and I were in her bedroom, and, as usual, I was reading her lessons aloud to her. We'd started with chemistry, where I had barely navigated through the thicket of the periodic table. (Molybdenum? Yttrium?) Now we were deep into our third hour of Advanced Placement world history and reviewing a chapter on Chinese history.

Sarah paced the room, repeating back key phrases about 3rd century B.C. China and orally summarizing the material, paragraph by paragraph. I made a wild stab at pronouncing the name of the emperor who united the warring provinces of China and built the Great Wall: Qin Shihuangdi. It came out like "Quincy Honky."

Sarah grabbed the book back. "That's not how my teacher pronounces it."

"Then you do it," I snapped.

Sarah burst into tears.

It's painful to recall, but the episode pushed us to discover and take advantage of powerful new technologies that eventually helped our oldest child achieve her full potential—that of a girl capable of plowing through difficult coursework and pulling down a 4.1 grade-point average.

Clues in First Grade

If only we could have foreseen the future in first grade, when we had our first inkling of a problem.

Back then, Sarah had a fondness for the book *Put Me in the Zoo*, not great literature but great fun to read when you're starting out on that voyage to literacy. She'd read the tale, about a funny, spotted leopard desperate for a home in the zoo, seemingly effortlessly, over and over again: "I would like to live this way. This is where I want to stay." At least, we thought she was reading it.

We soon discovered, when Sarah turned to other books, that she had been memorizing the words. Basic words such as "ball," "the" and "dog" baffled her. Sometimes she recognized words on one page but had no recall when she saw the words again a page later. At times, she reversed the order of words in sentences or skipped them entirely.

We brought up our concerns with her first-grade teacher. "You need to read to her more" was her response. But we were already reading heavily to Sarah. My husband and I are writers, and reading is a passion. We redoubled our efforts, recording the number of books on a log we kept on the kitchen table. Once a week, she took it to school, where the teacher put congratulatory stickers on it. By the end of the year, she'd hit 460 books.

Surely Sarah would pick up the ball and run with it, we thought. But while the other second-graders in her public school were sailing through, *The Magic School Bus* and *Amber Brown*—books with chapters, plots and complex thoughts—Sarah was stuck with basic readers such as *The Snowball.*

"I saw a snowball on a hill," it read. "It rolled along and picked up Bill!"

She read haltingly, stumbling over the simplest words. She surprised and baffled us by doing well on spelling tests, until we realized she was once again memorizing. Gradually, it dawned on Sarah, too, that there was a problem.

"Why can the other kids read better than me?" she asked us. We didn't know what to say. How do you reassure a child that her brain works fine—especially when you yourself don't know what the problem is? When Sarah was again placed in the lowest-level reading group in third grade, we decided to follow a friend's recommen-

FAST FACT

The Americans with Disabilities Act requires employers to make "reasonable accommodations" for applicants or workers with disabilities. These may include assistive technology for those with learning disabilities.

dation and, swallowing hard, shelled out $1,500 for a full battery of tests from an educational testing service.

IQ–Reading Ability Gap

Sarah turned out to be a classic dyslexic—among the 5 to 15 percent of schoolchildren with normal or above-average intelligence who perform significantly below their potential when handed a book or a pencil. One measure of dyslexia is a 15-point difference between IQ and reading achievement. Sarah had a 23-point gap.

To most people, a dyslexic is someone who reverses letters when he reads or writes. But dyslexia is not a deficit in the visual system. Dyslexics see words correctly. It is a deficit in the brain's language system—in the neurons that are used to process the distinctive sound elements that constitute language.

Dyslexics have a flawed ability to develop phonemic awareness—that is, the ability to divide the written word into its underlying segments, called phonemes. Phonemes are the smallest discernible segment of speech (for example, the word "cat" consists of three phonemes: kuh, aah, tuh) and the bedrock of reading. When learning to read, children naturally break apart each word into its phonemes and then rapidly reassemble it into a coherent word. Eventually, they learn to pay attention to the word's meaning rather than its sounds, and they read text rapidly, smoothly and effortlessly.

By contrast, dyslexics struggle to blend letter sounds to create whole words. For them, reading and spelling is like trying to crack an impossible code, and the effort can take a toll. Studies have shown that dyslexic students have significantly more academic and behavioral problems than children without learning disabilities. One 1996 study found that 2 percent of those with learning disabilities go on to a four-year college. Studies have also found that adult dyslexics have a lower satisfaction with health and friends, and exhibit more psychiatric problems than non-dyslexics. Fewer are employed and, even if employed, hold jobs that are part-time, minimum wage and unskilled. We spent Sarah's childhood in almost constant anxiety that our daughter, too, would spend her life as a frustrated underachiever.

But with the advent in the 1990s of functional brain imaging, technology began providing answers. To find the physical basis of "word blindness," researchers at four learning disability centers nationwide, among them the Center for the Study of Learning at Georgetown University, are using magnetic resonance imaging to map the neural pathways used in reading. By watching the brain as subjects read, researchers can track words and symbols as they bounce from the eyes to the visual cortex and through the circuitry of the brain.

In just the past few years, scans have revealed stunning details of what goes right—and wrong—when humans read. Scans have found that normal readers activate three interconnected neural systems in the brain's left hemisphere. Commonly seen words are directly processed in an area behind the left ear (the occipitotemporal cortex). The more complex work of picking apart words appears to be rooted in another area, above and slightly forward from there (the inferior parietal area).

A third area, just behind the left temple (called the inferior frontal gyrus), is responsible for analyzing word meaning and for the articulation of a word.

In dyslexics, the areas in the back, where words are formed and analyzed, aren't as engaged, while other areas, such as the front and the right side of the brain (used mostly for visual processing), become more active, perhaps as dyslexics struggle to compensate for the failure of their rear brain neural systems.

By taking thousands of images as dyslexic and normal readers identify letters flashing above them inside the glowing tunnel of the MRI, the Georgetown center and the other labs expect to soon determine whether intensive reading therapy can "rewire" the dyslexic brain. Eventually, they expect the research to lead to better diagnoses and treatment of dyslexia, perhaps before a child shows any signs of problems. In the meantime, there have been dramatic advancements in technologies that assist dyslexics in bridging the gap between their potential and their performance.

Improving Technology

During Sarah's elementary school years, such tools were helpful but rudimentary. After her diagnosis, she started using an electronic speller and a portable word-processing device so she could type her in-class assignments rather than handwrite them.

By seventh grade, she used a regular laptop, where spell-checker became a lifesaver.

By then, she had grasped the hard lessons of life as a dyslexic—that any task involving reading and writing would take her twice or three times as long as it took other kids. She went into victim mode, complaining that other kids had it too easy and that she was the only one who had to work so hard.

One day, she locked herself in the bathroom. "I'm dumb! I'm stupid!" she screamed through the door. "Those tests that said I was smart—they were wrong!"

In high school, concerned that she was sinking into a morass of self pity and anger, we had her retested by a private educational consultant, mostly to help her understand that her dyslexia was real. The results were the same. Her ability to blend sounds while reading, her reading fluency, her "word attack" (that is, her ability to process and sequence sounds) were far below average.

As we had requested, the consultant was blunt as she went through the results with my husband, me and Sarah. She ticked off Sarah's many strengths and then turned to her prospects for academic success. "You are never going to get a lot of A's," she told Sarah. "It wouldn't be fair to expect that of yourself. B's and C's are more realistic, and there's nothing wrong with that."

My husband and I were relieved. Maybe this would take the pressure off Sarah and reassure her that there was no shame in an average performance in school.

Sarah's face darkened. She nodded stiffly, and as soon as we were out the door, she turned on us furiously. "She's wrong," Sarah hissed at us. "I can so get A's. I'm going to get a 4.0."

Textbooks on Tape

Sarah signed up for honors-level and advanced placement classes at our public high school. She plunged into dense college-level textbooks and demanding writing assignments. But her laptop and Franklin speller couldn't keep up with the growing demands of her schoolwork. We ended up reading many of her assignments to her: a process that could take four hours or longer each night. Then came the outburst over the Chinese history lesson.

The next day, I found the Web site for Recording for the Blind and Dyslexic (RFB&D)—a nonprofit organization that produces recordings of books and textbooks for people with visual impairments and learning disabilities—and signed her up. The educational consultant we'd seen in third grade had suggested it, but I had always thought that Sarah could get by without it.

For decades, RFB&D issued its recordings on cassette tapes, a cumbersome process and bulky procedure that involved listening to as many as 10 cassettes for one book. But in 2002, the organization took a giant leap forward by introducing digitally recorded textbooks stored on CDs. With a special CD, Sarah could listen to her textbooks and skip around with a press of a button. To our surprise, RFB&D had a massive array of textbooks in stock—even science and French texts. The organization receives school curriculum lists from around the country, and volunteers record most books. The organization

will also take requests. We either ordered her books on-line or called the Washington office. The CDs, in a slim cardboard sleeve, showed up about a week later.

With the textbook recordings, Sarah could now do what most students do. She could move around a chapter or section, skipping or fast-forwarding through sections that she knew weren't relevant. She would curl up on her bed, earphones on, thumb on the buttons, looking at charts, maps and graphs as she read along, the words pouring into her ears. She also got Write: Out-loud, speech synthesizer software that read aloud what she wrote, reducing her endless hours of proofreading or relying on us to do it.

The CDs sliced an hour or so off her homework each night. The speech synthesizer improved her writing by letting her hear what she couldn't see. She could listen for missed words (she often left out conjunctions such as "or" and prepositions such as "on" or "by") and misused

Being able to listen to their textbooks on CDs, rather than merely reading, provides dyslexics with an efficient and time-saving method of study. (**Joe Raedle/Getty Images**)

words (frequently typing "their" instead of "the," and "you" instead of "your"). She was able to express more complete sentences and more complex thoughts.

But, far more important, the technology freed her from a dependence on others. She could now close the door of her room and do her homework on her own. It was still slow and painful. But it was her homework time, not our homework time.

Her math and English grades climbed from B's to A's. French moved from a B to a B+. History went from an occasional A to consistent A's. An English teacher who had noted early in the year that Sarah's sharp observations in class weren't reflected in her papers told us at the end of the year that Sarah's writing was much more fluid and, at times, even eloquent.

Dumb No More

Best of all, Sarah stopped referring to herself as "dumb" or "not as smart as the other kids in my class." Instead, she matter-of-factly told teachers and classmates that she had dyslexia. Now, it was a disorder she could name and see—and, with the technology, control. She made jokes about her chronic misspellings on e-mails and IMs. "What do you expect?" she said with a shrug to a friend after mangling the spelling in one. "I'm dyslexic."

In her junior year, she came up with a nickname for her sports jerseys, "Cixelsyd," ("dyslexic" spelled backward). A friend bought her a T-shirt with the slogan "Who put the sexy in dyslexic?"

Sarah's grades kept climbing. In her junior year, she reached her Holy Grail—a grade-point average for the year of 4.1.

As Sarah heads for college next year, assistive technology continues to develop. Among other tools, there are now $150 "reading pens," the size of a large felt-tip marker—hand-held text scanners that read aloud words or lines of text. Screen readers are now built into word-processing software to read information on the screen using synthesized speech. More advanced versions will read aloud the text on Web pages. And that's just the beginning.

Studies have shown that assistive technology improves the reading rate and comprehension of students with reading disabilities, improves their spelling and helps them find significantly more errors in their written compositions. One study found that college students with learning disabilities get higher writing scores when using speech recognition software than those who use a human transcriber or write without assistance. Just as important, it frees dyslexics such as Sarah from relying on someone else to learn, giving a boost to their self-confidence.

Will Sarah continue availing herself of all this new technology in college? She's still a stubborn teenager, so probably not at first.

But as her mother, I feel good knowing it's there whenever she needs it.

Learning to Learn Despite a Learning Disability

Kourtland R. Koch

In the following selection a professor of special education reveals his history of difficulties with education. Kourtland R. Koch grew up with learning disabilities that went undiagnosed until he was nearly an adult. From his first days in elementary school, Koch struggled to conform to behavioral expectations and to read. Expelled from Catholic school, he was held back in public school and placed in the lowest readers group. His self-esteem plummeted. However, he found some redemption in highly structured clubs and camps, where he felt on equal footing with other boys. Eventually, he was placed in a special remedial school that applied advanced diagnostic and teaching methods best suited to a young man with learning disabilities. There, with the help of a mentor, he discovered a love of learning that led him to a university career. Kourtland R. Koch is an associate professor of special education at Ball State University in Muncie, Indiana.

SOURCE: Kourtland R. Koch, "Learning to Learn Despite LD: A Personal Story," *Teaching Exceptional Children Plus,* vol. 1, September 2004. Copyright © 2004 by Kourtland R. Koch. Republished with permission of Council for Exceptional Children, conveyed through Copyright Clearance Center, Inc.

I was not identified as a person with learning disabilities until the eleventh grade. Prior to that time, I had an extremely humiliating, frustrating, and socially and emotionally painful educational experience. My story will be familiar to many individuals with learning disabilities. My goal is that my educational life experience with learning disabilities will become a story unique to the past. This goal will only be realized by making available effective strategies, tools, and remedies to teachers, specialists, administrators, and families of individuals with learning disabilities. I hope my story will provide insights and helpful specifics to educators, parents, and individuals who struggle to teach and to learn despite the presence of learning disabilities. Indeed, a student's biggest hope for success depends upon the quality of instruction and interventions received.

Conflict at Catholic School

I entered first grade at Saint Anthony's Catholic School, where my mother was a teacher. However, due to my uncontrollable behavior in the classroom, the monsignor informed my parents I would not be allowed to continue my education at St. Anthony's. As a result, my parents had no choice but to enroll me in the local public school the following year.

Though I was a behavior problem, I do not think my parents began to understand the magnitude of my difficulties until I was asked to leave the Catholic school. I was retained at the end of second grade. I could not sit still and was disruptive in class. Standing in the hallway for 15 to 20 minutes at a time became commonplace, as did trips to the principal's office when I was discovered wandering the halls. I was paddled so often that the consequence lost meaning.

My misbehavior provoked numerous parent-teacher conferences that always ended with my promising that

I would do better. Despite my good intentions, no one ever provided me with any strategies for actually doing better and neither my behavior, nor academic performance improved.

Reading Challenges

My written expression grades were dismal, reflecting only the quality of my illegible handwriting, rather than my story content or grammar usage. I was placed in the lowest reading group, the Black Birds, and I felt like a crow—a nuisance bird. Blue Birds and Red Birds received more attention from the teacher. They were assigned fun, creative projects. Our instructional time was limited, and the expectations for the Black Birds were minimal at best. We were "taught" to read using the "look-say" method well characterized by the popular *Dick and Jane* series of the time. But, reading never became easy for me. Even now, as a professional educator, reading is not something I have ever learned to enjoy.

Changing schools had not modified my behavior. As time passed, I continued to be penalized for poor self-control. Still, no positive interventions were forthcoming. Without question, I had become the victim of a self-fulfilling prophecy. My behavior problems continued, and I began falling further and further behind my classmates academically. My self-esteem suffered and I misbehaved more. My teachers perceived me as a poor student. I was living up to every negative impression and expectation they formed for me. My parents and my teachers continued to believe that telling me what I was doing wrong would be enough to straighten me out. What I still lacked and needed was specific and explicit instruction about how to do things "right." I recall my early school years as a critical time for my family filled with confusion, devastation, frustration, anger, concern, and stress.

Boost from Boys Club

After I entered third grade, my mother attempted to boost my self-esteem by enrolling me in the Boys Club. It was the first winning strategy I was given. At the Boys Club, I found a place where I could excel. Participation in football, basketball, and baseball gave me my first, much-needed sense of success. Soon, I lived only to go to the Boys Club and longed not to attend school where I was miserable. With good intentions my mother made attendance at the Boys Club dependent on success and good behavior in school. As high as my motivation was, the skills I needed to succeed in school failed to appear magically. This new behavior plan proved to be disheartening.

My mom stumbled upon a second winning strategy when she enrolled me in a Catholic youth camp. I was to spend eight weeks at camp each summer until I was 13. At summer camp, learning became fun for the very first

Organized activities such as those offered at local Boys & Girls Clubs can help children excel and give them a sense of self-worth. (Juan Ocampo/ NBAE via Getty Images)

time. Sister Elizabeth understood how much I wanted to become an altar boy. She worked hard with me so that I could meet my goal. With her help, I memorized the Catholic mass through repetition. She drew pictures on the blackboard to show me where to go. Then we rehearsed my part until it was flawless. I was motivated to learn, given strategies to succeed, and rewarded for my effort. I had earned the privilege of becoming an altar boy.

Having Structure Helps

Catholic youth camp was highly structured and predictable. This structure enabled me to anticipate the camp schedule, putting me on an equal footing with other campers. I was prepared, because I always knew what to expect next. With each passing year, I gained status and added responsibility as an experienced camper. My self-esteem increased, helping to orient new campers developed my leadership skills.

The single most important intervention summer camp provided was a consistent relationship with loving and caring adults who learned how to work with me over the years. I attribute my growing confidence and self-esteem during my elementary years to summer camp. Each year, I felt a little better about myself. Eventually, I started to believe that I was smart and capable of success.

In spite of my growing success at camp each summer, my parents did not recognize a need to intervene on my behalf at school. During the 1960's, parents continued to trust the school system to address my academic and behavioral needs. However, I was the child who was left further and further behind in school. No one, my parents, teachers, or administrators, really understood why. It was assumed that I was not trying hard enough, or that I was just plain lazy, or a problem child. These natural presumptions meant that teachers were prone to spend their time and energy on more worthy students.

By the end of elementary school, not only was I struggling in reading, but math was also becoming a real challenge. I could not understand math, so I did not enjoy it. The only subjects I did like in elementary school were science and social studies. I was interested in animals, planets, and history. I was also able to perform the activities that the science curriculum entailed because science was highly structured. My social studies teacher would show us movies and bring in guest speakers. Learning these two subjects did not depend on my reading or math ability. Consequently, they were subjects I could master or at least not fail.

Termed "at Risk"

By the 7th grade, I had been labeled an "at-risk" low academic achiever. I had still never been tested or diagnosed formally. Clearly, the expectations were lower for a poorer performing student. I was placed into a vocational education track and away from the academic track intended for students bound for post-secondary education. The vocational curriculum emphasized essential job skills such as punctuality, dependability, and getting along with employers, customers, and peers.

The vocational program was a way of addressing the needs of students, like me, who were perceived as at-risk of dropping out of school. In retrospect, many of my friends in the program did leave high school without a diploma, remained unemployed or underemployed, and were dependent upon their families for support. Additionally, establishing successful, functional relationships was a problem many of us faced. We lacked social skills and struggled to "read" people or social situations properly. With hindsight, it is now easy to surmise that many of my classmates in the vocational education program may have also been identified as learning disabled. Many students were of low socio-economic status, which was also an indicator of vocationally tracked students.

A Tragic Change

Halfway through seventh grade, I began living with friends of my parents while my mom was away from home with my father seeking medical treatment for his cancer. Our family had a new crisis, and it was not my school performance. Before the school year was finished, my father would be dead. While I was born into a well-off family, my father's death meant that our socio-economic status plummeted. My mom had to resume working, and I had to enter the work force to help make ends meet. I had joined the ranks of the truly at-risk students. All unnecessary expenses were cut and thereby compounding my loss, this included my involvement in the Boys Club and summer camp.

Prior to my father's death, I belonged in the "preppies" clique, even though academically I belonged with the outcast and misfit kids. In effect, I was able to play both worlds and associate with whomever served my needs at any particular time. However, there was no escape from the misfit label once I became poor. I was an outcast no longer by choice, but because that was now my sole social and academic identity.

My vocational education track included a school-to-work program. I left school each day to work the lunch shift at McDonald's restaurant. I learned valuable work skills, earned money for my family during school hours, and within my first year was named an Employee of the Month. The rewards were high, but not without costs. My academic instruction was limited to just 3 1/2 hours per day. I was performing academically below my grade level, yet it was impossible to catch up with my general education peers who were receiving twice the instruction that I received. At school, my self-esteem spiraled downward.

FAST FACT

In 1975 Congress enacted the Education for All Handicapped Children Act (Public Law 94-142) to support states and localities in protecting the rights of, meeting the individual needs of, and improving the results for children with learning disabilities or other impediments to education.

A Change of Schools

My high school had no school-to-work program. I was again placed in a full academic curriculum. I was wholly unprepared. Yet, I knew I was a better student than people perceived me to be academically and than I was able to demonstrate. It was frustrating to be an academic and social outcast because I believed I was capable of more. I began to search actively for a place where I could fit. During my junior year, my mother suffered a nervous breakdown and a neighbor, Uncle John, became my guardian. Uncle John enrolled me in The Mills School, a nearby boarding school for children who had difficulty learning. The premise of the Mills School was to develop a remediation plan for each student according to their individual learning styles and make accommodations and modifications in instruction as necessary based upon observations, trial lessons, and accurate assessment. I was now almost 18 years old. Just as I was about to finish secondary school, I was to embark upon a new, long, and remarkable educational journey. A knowledgeable guardian, some self-advocacy, and the professional educators who truly understood learning disabilities made this possible.

A Love of Learning

The Mills School developed a remediation plan for me (a forerunner of the present-day IEP [Individual Education Plan]), based upon the results of a psycho-educational assessment. The evaluation identified learning styles and reading methods to increase my reading comprehension and overall academic success. The school psychologist employed selective behavioral techniques to teach me self-discipline, effective study habits, and a love for learning. These interventions worked. One teacher in particular, Mr. B., made learning an adventure with learning centers and high interest materials and incentives, such as listening to the radio or brewing coffee during class.

The Mills School provided me with a perceptive group of teachers for the first time in my life. I had the good fortune to interact with several outstanding, recognized professionals at the height of their careers in special education and school psychology. These teachers were concerned about my welfare and my future success. They believed I could learn, if only they would teach effectively. I began to seek these teachers out and found them. Several of these teachers have actually worked with me for a lifetime. These long-term relationships have offered stability and support for my academic endeavors first as a student, next as a public school teacher and administrator, and now as a university professor.

Evaluation, assessment, and diagnosis of my learning disabilities afforded me the opportunity to benefit from the same curriculum as the general education population. It was finally understood that I was capable and that I could succeed to the same degree as any student. With diagnosis, I was able to receive necessary accommodations and modifications which would allow me to earn the highest educational degree available in my field—something which would never have been possible if my learning disabilities had remained undiscovered.

A College Student Recounts His Brother's Battle with Asperger's Syndrome

Cristof Traudes

In the selection that follows, undergraduate Cristof Traudes tells the agonizing tale of his bright but stricken older brother Erik. As Traudes tells it, Erik excels at math and has a positive genius for recollecting sports trivia. Yet he struggled in school and frequently spent long nights in tears over his frustration. Erik, Traudes explains, suffers from Asperger's syndrome, a neurological disorder that lies on the mild end of the autistic spectrum. One of its symptoms is intense obsessions, and in Erik's case this manifested itself in sports and science fiction. He also exhibited an unusually impulsive, self-centered, and highly emotional nature that made it hard to make friends or concentrate in school. As a result, despite being highly intelligent, Erik struggled in school. The story has a relatively happy ending, however. Both brothers graduated from high school and made it to college.

Traudes was a student at the University of Missouri when he wrote this piece. Today he works as a journalist in Minnesota's Twin Cities, Minneapolis-Saint Paul.

SOURCE: Cristof Traudes, "A Brother's Story," *Columbia Missourian*, March 10, 2007. Reproduced by permission.

I celebrated my 21st birthday last fall at a Tex-Mex restaurant north of downtown Columbia. The walls were mounted with "genuine" sombreros and large TVs tuned to ESPN. I was happy with the combination of friends who gathered—there were friends I played with in Marching Mizzou, friends from the journalism school, friends from high school.

And there was my brother, Erik, 24. He sat to my left, wearing the bright red Minnesota Twins T-shirt I had scored for him during my summer work there. It was pretty special—not every kid gets to have his big brother at his milestone birthday.

I spent a lot of the night talking to the people in my corner—my brother Erik; friends Mark, Tom, Buddy and Aaron. I turned to Buddy, an MU music student who's been one of my best friends since our days at West Junior High School.

How's it going? I asked. *Classes and everything OK?*

Yeah, Buddy said. *Just the usual music school thing. Lots of practicing, lots of rehearsals. You?*

It's going well, I said. *I—*

Erik interrupted me midsentence. *Did you see that Georgia Tech is beating Virginia?!*

Really? I said to him. *Interesting. . . .*

Neither team meant much to me. I turned back to Buddy. *I—*

Whoa! Erik blurted out. *Did you see the Twins' score?*

I glanced up at the TV. The Twins had lost another game that could've ensured them postseason play. Oh well. I turned back to Buddy. *I—*

Did you— Erik again, jumping in from my left. I tried to ignore him.

—am doing well. The J-School—

Did you—

—is keeping me—

Whoa! Did you—

I never finished my conversation with Buddy. But that's a given when Erik's around. It's always been that way.

But it's barely been a year since I understood why.

My brother has Asperger's syndrome.

Erik and I both stand 5 feet l0 inches tall. We're both relatively skinny, although he's starting to develop a little gut. We've both worked at Schnucks grocery store as baggers and cashiers for more than four years, often on the same shift. And despite our three-year difference in age, we're both seniors at MU [University of Missouri] scheduled to graduate in May.

The similarities end there. . . .

A Mysterious Condition

When my friends meet Erik, his rapid-fire knowledge first impresses, then baffles and, finally, annoys. But after trying to signal with yawns, frowns and turned heads that they're ready to stop listening, he just keeps talking.

That's usually the point when they come to me and ask why my brother is so weird. For years, I secretly asked myself the same question.

Now I can tell them he has Asperger's syndrome, a "mild" neurological disorder in the same spectrum as autism. That puts Erik in fast-growing company; as many as one in 150 children in America suffer from some form of autism, according to a study released in February [2007] by the Centers for Disease Control [and Prevention].

What I don't often tell friends is that Erik's obsessions are just one characteristic of his condition. They don't know how much he struggled in school despite his superior intelligence. They don't know about the long nights of crying, or that his mysterious and stubborn behavior strained my family to a breaking point. They don't know that we lived with this mystery for 23 years, not knowing what caused it and when—or if—it would end.

The world of psychology is almost as much in the dark about these aspects of Asperger's. It acknowledged the disorder's existence little more than a decade ago; research remains in the discovery phase.

Some things about Asperger's are generally known. For example, its symptoms vary greatly from person to person. Some might have obsessive routines, or sensitivity to bright lights and loud sounds. Others have major motor-skill problems or are considered "little professors" because of a precocious formal speaking style.

Asperger's is five times as likely to appear in males as it is in females. Like all forms of autism, it is being diagnosed at an increasing rate in both children and adults. It stands out because it's a "high-functioning" disorder, usually not accompanied by problems with language development or similar learning skills.

The most universal aspect of Asperger's, however, isn't a scientific fact. Rather, it's what makes its label as a "mild" disorder sadly ironic. It's the social side: Most of those with Asperger's have normal intelligence and verbal skills, but their fixation on select topics makes it hard for them to take part in the give-and-take of regular conversation.

As children, people with Asperger's tend to get bullied. As adults, they often get labeled as weird and have trouble in the job market while they struggle at maintaining relationships. . . .

Trouble in School

An IQ test administered by the MU Assessment and Consultation Clinic in 2006 placed Erik in the 99th percentile compared to others in his age group. Still, school was never easy for him.

We had moved to Columbia a year earlier, in 1998, to be closer to Mom's family. Erik and I had to leave our Dutch roots behind and adopt American culture. But I was mostly excited. I could refresh my image, make it whatever I wanted it to be. It would be a time for reinvention.

For Erik, there was no reinvention. Just recurrence.

On the surface, Hickman High School was refreshing for him. As one of 2,000-plus students, he found it easier to blend into the background there, which enabled him to stop being a target for bullies. He also found people who shared his passion for the fantasy card game "Magic: The Gathering." Playing cards masked his social awkwardness.

But the high of having friends at school was a stark contrast to the despair he felt at home. . . .

Lying in my tiny, neat room—separated from my brother by one wall—I listened to Erik's reality and realized I was becoming the older brother.

The tears usually started around 11 P.M. or midnight. Mom would come from down the hallway, the hardwood floor creaking under her feet.

"What's wrong?" she'd ask.

"I just—I just—can't, you know," I'd hear Erik mumble. Sniffles would interrupt and garble his words. His unfinished homework would lie on his cluttered desk like an accusation. I can't.

"Sure you can," my mom would urge.

"I just—I just—I . . ."

He explained it to me recently, the difficulty he has with schoolwork. His mind wants to start wandering as soon as he sits down. Once he finally gets focused, it takes only the smallest snag, whether it's a question that's too hard or a little worry that his essay won't be the best in the class, to set his mind off again.

He'd hit snag after snag until, around midnight, he'd realize he wouldn't be able to finish the assignment. And that bothered him, because he'd always considered himself a prime student.

"I never have been able to effectively sit down and just do homework," he said. ". . . I can write well. I'm a good writer. I just can't sit down and do it."

Many with Asperger's have a similar experience. . . . The problem can be compounded in the classroom. While most teachers know how to deal with students who don't want to do homework, they aren't always as prepared to deal with those who want to but can't because of a mental block. . . .

For me, Erik's educational lapses created a dark understanding: I would eclipse my older brother—the older brother whose fantasy world I once thrived in, the older brother I grew up wanting to be like.

Hearing him cry through the wall was also the first time I felt complete empathy for him.

The second time was when he flunked out of MU.

Ascent and Descent

Erik walked across the stage of the Hearnes Center on June 3, 2000, wearing the bright purple gown and mortarboard of Hickman High. He flashed the wide-open grin of his childhood. "I was really happy," he told me. "I knew I was going to be going to college. It was going to kick ass and I was going to be out in four years."

Statistics were against him. Deborah Wright, clinic director at the MU Assessment and Consultation Clinic, said many students with Asperger's syndrome take eight to nine years to finish college. Others drop out entirely.

Erik started at MU as a computer science major intending to program his own video games one day. He moved into a dormitory. He and his roommate had little in common and barely talked.

It was one of the happiest times of his life. He could play video games without getting so absorbed in them that his schoolwork faltered. His depression was receding, despite having little social interaction. At fall's end, his grade-point average was 3.579 out of a possible 4.

Spring semester was different.

Erik was still happy. He was making a slew of new friends. All of them were deeply interested in video games and seemed to spend all of their time playing them—just as Erik wanted to do. He even started dating. It was a social high point for the former boy in the corner.

But Erik's mind was where it had always been. While he thought his friends played video games 24/7, they were able to set them aside for the two to three hours they needed to do homework. When time came for Erik to do the same, the added social distractions made him forget his priorities.

His grade point plunged to 1.136. Seven months later, it was 0.900. MU booted him.

He moved back home. He worked part time at the grocery store. He lost his pride, his joy and his hope. He took a deep plunge back into depression. The former nights spent in anguish about high school homework were nothing compared to these months worrying about his future.

"They say you can accomplish whatever you set your mind to," Erik said to me recently, eyebrows tightened together. "Setting my mind to it isn't enough. You also have to set effort to it. But when I hit a snag, that was it." . . .

> ## FAST FACT
>
> The essential symptoms of Asperger's syndrome are sustained impairment in social interaction and the development of restricted, repetitive patterns of behavior, interests, and activities. In contrast to autism, there are no significant delays in acquiring language.

Trying Again

They were scary times, those months after Erik flunked out of MU. The questions we asked ourselves were even scarier. Could Erik ever earn a college degree? And even if he could, would it matter? Would he be able to thrive—or survive—on his own?

"I can picture Erik being a street person," Mom told me. "I mean the classic one you find living under a bridge who's brilliant and who's writing some mathematical problem or some absolutely brilliant poetry."

We didn't want that to happen. Erik didn't want that to happen. He wanted back into MU.

Together with Mom and Dad, he searched for a way. They found it after numerous meetings with advisers and officials. Within half a year, in the fall of 2002, Erik was a Tiger again. "It felt wonderful," he said.

But this time, Erik lived at home. Mom and Dad kept an eye on his schedule and made sure he didn't lose hours, days, weeks. Erik also had to pay for every class in which he scored lower than a B.

The first semester back, his lowest grade was a B-plus. During the three semesters he spent living at home, his lowest GPA was 3.657. His highest was 4.0.

With success in sight—and having a kid brother who now lived on campus—Erik earned his way back into the dorms.

His old friends were still there—the ones who loved video games and science fiction, just like him. His grades dropped slightly, but this time Erik was aware of it happening, and he maintained control. The return was blissful.

Unfortunately, with every high, there is a low. Erik slumped again, slipping into depression whenever he wasn't as good as he wanted to be.

At the beginning of 2006, Erik turned to the MU Assessment and Consultation Clinic. He took test after test after test. Asperger's soon became a household name for us.

It took 23 years, but we finally had a clear reason for why Erik had been the boy in the corner, why he couldn't stop talking about baseball and video games, why homework was such a challenge, why he'd gone through everything he had.

Diagnosed—and Labeled

For Erik, the diagnosis was a mixed blessing. "It was kind of a relief," he said. "It's nice to have something to say, but there is the whole deal of being labeled the rest of my life."

For Mom and Dad, they finally had an enemy they could battle and a reason their exhaustive parenting didn't work.

As for me, I now had an answer for people who ask why my brother is so weird, why he won't shut up. His diagnosis gave me a chance to teach. It also gave me a bit of tolerance for the times Erik would shift our conversations from real-life problems to why my Minnesota Twins cap has the letters "T" and "C" instead of an "M," or how the state of Arizona has mixed emotions about the Diamondbacks switching their team colors from purple and green to red and black.

An Uncertain Future

Getting a medical diagnosis meant gaining understanding that there are others out there like Erik— that he isn't alone in the world. And somewhere out there are other little brothers and sisters who grew up with the same littler-but-older sensation I've had for years—a sensation that secretly made me feel like a jerk.

We're twins again. Graduation is coming up soon for both of us. There are new things to worry about, like which ceremony Mom and Dad will attend and how they'll make it up to the son they'll be snubbing. (Erik and I will graduate from different schools in different buildings at about the same time.)

But that's one day's logistic. This is the rest of life: What's next for Erik?

Really, who knows?

GLOSSARY

accommodations	With reference to disabilities, techniques and materials that facilitate learning and help individuals with a learning disorder to complete school or work tasks with greater ease and effectiveness. Examples include spell-checkers, tape recorders, and expanded time for completing assignments.
age-equivalent score	A score that indicates what an average child of a certain age would be expected to achieve.
Americans with Disabilities Act (ADA)	A federal law that gives civil rights protections affording equal opportunity for individuals with disabilities in public accommodations, employment, transportation, state and local government services, and telecommunications.
assessment	The systematic evaluation and documentation of a student's ability or performance in a particular area.
assistive technology	Equipment that enhances the ability of people with disabilities to be more efficient and successful.
attention deficit disorder (ADD)	A neurological condition marked by severe difficulty in concentraing and maintaining attention. Often used synonymously with atention deficit/hyperactivity disorder. (See next entry.)
attention deficit hyperactivity disorder (ADHD)	A range of behavioral disorders characterized by symptoms that include poor concentration, an inability to focus on tasks, difficulty in paying attention, and impulsivity.
auditory discrimination	The ability to distinguish one kind of sound from another, such as the sounds of various phonemes.
decoding	The ability to translate a word from print to speech, usually by employing knowledge of sound-symbol correspondences. It is also the act of deciphering a new word by sounding it out.

dyscalculia	A disability that creates severe difficulty in comprehending, processing, or using mathematical symbols or functions.
dyslexia	A neurological condition that causes severe difficulty in processing language, including listening, speaking, reading, writing, and spelling.
dysnomia	An exceptional difficulty in remembering names or recalling words needed for oral or written language.
formative assessment	Assessments designed to evaluate students on a frequent basis so that adjustments can be made in instruction to help them reach their goals.
grade-equivalent scores	A score that is expressed in terms of what grade an average student achieving that score would be in.
individualized education program (IEP)	A plan outlining special education and related services specifically designed to meet the unique educational needs of a student with a disability.
integration	The mental process in which various types of information and sensory input are brought together in the brain.
learning disability	A neurological disorder that interferes with a person's ability to learn or forces them to learn in a way different from the average person.
learning styles	Approaches to instruction that focus on the variations in student temperament, attitude, and comfort in learning.
mainstream	A term denoting the standard, typical, or average educational setting or student.
multisensory structured language education	An educational approach that combines visual, auditory, and tactile input to enhance learning.
resource program	An instructional plan in which a learning disabled student spends time in a regular classroom for most of each day but also receives specialized services addressing the disability.

specific language disability	A severe difficulty in some aspect of listening, speaking, reading, writing, or spelling.
visual discrimination	The perceptual ability to distinguish letters and words that may appear similar.
word attack skills	The ability to decode words through knowledge of the sound-symbol correspondence of the language.
word decoding	A process for identifying and interpreting written symbols as words.

CHRONOLOGY

1853 Pennsylvania establishes the Pennsylvania Training School for Feeble-Minded Children, a school for children with intellectual disabilities.

1876 Physician Edouard Seguin becomes the first president of the Association of Medical Officers of American Institutions for Idiotic and Feebleminded Persons, which evolves into the American Association on Intellectual and Developmental Disabilities.

1877 German neurologist Adolf Kussamaul coins the term *word blindness,* a precursor to dyslexia.

1887 German physician Rudolf Berlin applies the term *dyslexia* to a recognized inability to interpret written or printed symbols.

1902 British pediatrician George Frederick Still describes cases of hyperactive children whom he believes can be diagnosed with an underlying medical condition.

1905 Cleveland ophthalmologist W.E. Bruner publishes the first U.S. report of childhood reading difficulties.

1921 James Sorenson is born into poverty and dyslexia, which he eventually overcomes to become a billionaire inventor.

1935 Psychiatrist Samuel T. Orton and educator Anna Gillingham invent a multisensory method of teaching dyslexic children to read. It becomes known as the Orton-Gillingham method.

1937 Psychiatrist Charles Bradley experiments with the use of stimulants to treat hyperactive children.

1956 Ritalin is introduced as a treatment for hyperactive children.

1963 Educator and psychologist Samuel A. Kirk becomes the first person to use the term *learning disability,* at a conference in Chicago.

1969 Congress passes the Children with Specific Learning Disabilities Act, which mandates for the first time support services for students with learning disabilities.

1974 A study conducted in Florida finds evidence that fluorescent lighting in schools can alter the behavior of hyperactive children.

1975 The Education for All Handicapped Children Act requires a free, appropriate public education for all students.

1980 The term *attention deficit disorder* (ADD) gains official recognition.

1987 The American Psychiatric Association updates the term ADD to *attention deficit hyperactivity disorder* (ADHD).

1990 Congress passes the Individuals with Disabilities Education Act (IDEA), incorporating and building on earlier legislation.

1997 The number of children being treated for attention deficit hyperactivity disorder passes 1 million. The condition is added to the list that makes children eligible for special education.

2004 IDEA is reauthorized, bringing it into alignment with the No Child Left Behind Act.

ORGANIZATIONS TO CONTACT

The editors have compiled the following list of organizations concerned with the issues debated in this book. The descriptions are derived from materials provided by the organizations. All have publications or information available for interested readers. The list was compiled on the date of publication of the present volume; the information provided here may change. Be aware that many organizations take several weeks or longer to respond to inquiries, so allow as much time as possible.

Association on Higher Education and Disability (AHEAD)
107 Commerce Center Dr., Ste. 204
Huntersville, NC 28078 USA
(704) 947-7779
fax: (704) 948-7779
www.ahead.org

AHEAD seeks full participation in higher education for persons with disabilities. It promotes excellence through education, communication, and training. It also produces publications, including the *Journal of Postsecondary Education and Disability*.

Attention Deficit Disorder Association (ADDA)
PO Box 7557
Wilmington, DE 19803-9997
phone/fax: (800) 939-1019
www.add.org

The ADDA provides information, resources, and networking opportunities to help adults with attention deficit hyperactivity disorder (ADHD) lead better lives. A nonprofit organization, it educates the public and advocates for legislation to advance the interests of people with ADHD.

Children and Adults with Attention Deficit/Hyperactivity Disorder (CHADD)
8181 Professional Pl.
Ste. 150
Landover, MD 20785
(301) 306-7070
(800) 233-4050
fax: (301) 306-7090
www.chadd.org

CHADD works to improve the lives of people affected by ADHD through collaborative leadership, advocacy, research, education, and support. It serves as a national resource center on ADHD. It has health information specialists who are available to members, professionals, and the general public to answer questions about ADHD and to provide referrals to local chapters and other community resources.

Council for Exceptional Children (CEC)
1110 North Glebe Rd.
Ste. 300
Arlington, VA 22201
(703) 620-3660
(888) 232-7733
(866) 915-5000 TTY
fax: (703) 264-9494
www.cec.sped.org

The CEC focuses on the educational success of children with disabilities and children who are gifted and talented and supports the professionals who serve them. It conducts conferences and programs on special and gifted education, publishes journals and newsletters on current research and special education topics, develops and implements standards for special education and gifted programs, and advocates for effective policies and legislation for special and gifted education.

Council for Learning Disabilities (CLD)
PO Box 4014
Leesburg, VA 20177
(571) 258-1010
fax: (571) 258-1011
www.cldinternational
.org

The CLD promotes effective teaching and research to enhance the education and lifespan development of individuals with learning disabilities. It establishes standards of excellence and promotes strategies for research and practice through interdisciplinary collegiality, collaboration, and advocacy. It also publishes the *Learning Disability Quarterly*.

International Dyslexia Association (IDA)
40 York Rd., 4th Fl.
Baltimore, MD 21204
(410) 296-0232
(800) 222-3123
fax: (410) 321-5069
www.interdys.org

The IDA is the oldest nonprofit, scientific, and educational organization dedicated to the study and treatment of dyslexia. It also researches related language-based learning differences.

Learning Disabilities Association of America (LDA)
4156 Library Rd.
Pittsburgh, PA 15234-1349
(412) 341-1515
fax: (412) 344-0224
www.ldanatl.org

The LDA has provided support to people with learning disabilities since 1963. It also works with parents, teachers, and other professionals. At the national, state, and local levels, LDA provides cutting-edge information on learning disabilities, practical solutions, and a comprehensive network of resources. These services make the association the leading resource for information on learning disabilities.

National Association for Adults with Special Learning Needs
4380 Forbes Blvd.
Lanham, MD 20706
(800) 496-9222
www.naasln.com

The National Association for Adults with Special Learning Needs advocates for national policy, legislation, and funding to support adults with special learning needs. The group provides professional development and technical assistance and disseminates information and research. It works to increase awareness of holistic services and of the best practices for serving adults with special learning needs.

National Association for the Education of African American Children with Learning Disabilities
PO Box 09521
Columbus, OH 43209
(614) 237-6021
fax: (614) 238-0929
www.aacld.org

The National Association for the Education of African American Children with Learning Disabilities seeks to improve the quality of education for African American children by raising the level of awareness in their communities about learning differences. It promotes an understanding among parents, educators, and others of the culturally sensitive issues facing minority children with learning disabilities as defined by federal law. It also serves as a clearinghouse of information and resources for parents, African American educators, and others responsible for providing an appropriate education for students.

National Center for Learning Disabilities (NCLD)
381 Park Ave. S.
Ste. 1401
New York, NY 10016
(212) 545-7510
fax: (212) 545-9665
www.ncld.org

The NCLD is a nonprofit organization that works to ensure that U.S. children, adolescents, and adults with learning disabilities have the opportunity to succeed in school, work, and life.

National Dissemination Center for Children with Disabilities (NICHCY)
PO Box 1492
Washington, DC
20013-1492
(800) 695-0285 voice and TTY
fax: (202) 884-8441
www.nichcy.org

The NICHCY acts as a central source of information on disabilities in infants, toddlers, and children and on federal laws affecting those with disabilities. It also connects interested persons with research-based information on effective educational practices.

National Institute of Child Health and Human Development (NICHD)
National Institutes of Health, DHHS
31 Center Dr.
Rm. 2A32, MSC 2425
Bethesda, MD 20892-2425
(301) 496-5133
fax: (301) 496-7101
www.nichd.nih.gov

The NICHD was established to investigate human development as a means of understanding developmental disabilities, including mental retardation, and the events that occur during pregnancy. Today, the institute conducts and supports research on all stages of human development, from preconception to adulthood, to better understand the health of children, adults, families, and communities.

National Institute of Mental Health (NIMH)
Office of Communications
6001 Executive Blvd.
Rm. 8184, MSC 9663
Bethesda, MD 20892-9663
(301) 443-4513
(866) 615-6464
(301) 443-8431 TTY
fax: (301) 443-4279
www.nimh.nih.gov

The NIMH provides information concerning mental illness and behavior disorders, including attention deficit hyperactivity disorder. The federal agency conducts research on mind, brain, and behavior and offers a variety of publications in English and Spanish.

National Rehabilitation Information Center (NARIC)
8201 Corporate Dr.
Ste. 600
Landover, MD 20785
(301) 459-5900
(800) 346-2742
(301) 459-5984 TTY
fax: (301) 459-4263
www.naric.com

The NARIC serves as an information center focusing on a wide range of disability and rehabilitation issues. It houses a collection of disability and rehabilitation research literature, both federally funded and commercially produced. Information specialists provide information and referral free of charge and document delivery and customized database searches for nominal fees.

FOR FURTHER READING

Books

Teri James Bellis, *When the Brain Can't Hear: Unraveling the Mystery of Auditory Processing Disorder.* New York: Simon & Schuster, 2002.

Dale S. Brown, *Learning a Living: A Guide to Planning Your Career and Finding a Job for People with Learning Disabilities, Attention Deficit Disorder, and Dyslexia.* Bethesda, MD: Woodbine House, 2000.

S. Chinn and R. Ashcroft, *Mathematics for Dyslexics: A Teaching Handbook.* 2nd ed. London: Whurr, 1998.

Christopher Green and Kit Chee, *Understanding ADHD: The Definitive Guide to Attention Deficit Hyperactivity Disorder.* New York: Ballantine, 1998.

Lorraine Hammond, *When Bright Kids Fail: How to Help Children Overcome Specific Learning Difficulties.* New York: Simon & Schuster, 1998.

Joan M. Harwell, *Complete Learning Disabilities Handbook,* 2nd ed. San Francisco: Jossey Bass, 2001.

Lesley Hughes and Paul Cooper, *Understanding and Supporting Children with ADHD: Strategies for Teachers, Parents and Other Professionals.* Thousand Oaks, CA: Paul Chapman, 2007.

The International Dyslexia Association, *Basic Facts About Dyslexia: What Everyone Ought to Know,* 3rd ed. Baltimore: International Dyslexia Association, 2002.

Lynn Kern Koegel and Claire LaZebnik, *Growing Up on the Spectrum: A Guide to Life, Love, and Learning for Teens and Young Adults with Autism and Asperger's.* New York: Viking, 2009.

National Institute of Mental Health, *A Look at Attention Deficit Hyperactivity Disorder.* Bethesda, MD: National Institute of Mental Health, 2004.

Gavin Reid and Shannon Green, *100 Ideas for Supporting Pupils with Dyslexia*. New York: Continuum, 2007.

Sandra F. Rief, *The Dyslexia Checklist: A Practical Reference for Parents and Teachers*. San Francisco: Jossey-Bass, 2010.

Arlyn J. Roffman, *Meeting the Challenge of Learning Disabilities in Adulthood*. Baltimore: Paul H. Brookes, 2000.

Corinne Smith and Lisa Strick, *Learning Disabilities A to Z*. New York: Free Press, 1997.

Sally Smith, *No Easy Answers: The Learning Disabled Child at Home and at School*. New York: Bantam, 1995.

Periodicals and Internet Sources

Aliyeh Baruchin, "Attention Deficits That May Linger Well Past Childhood," *New York Times*, March 12, 2008.

David Brown, "Mental Activity May Affect Autism-Linked Genes," *Washington Post*, July 11, 2008.

J. Carroll and J. Iles, "An Assessment of Anxiety Levels in Dyslexic Students in Higher Education," *British Journal of Educational Psychology*, vol. 76, 2006.

John T. Chambers, interview by the *New York Times*, "In a Near-Death Event, a Corporate Rite of Passage," August 1, 2009.

R.A. Figueroa and P. Newsome, "The Diagnosis of LD in English Language Learners: Is It Nondiscriminatory?" *Journal of Learning Disabilities*, vol. 39, no. 3, 2006.

Scott Howard, "Neurobiology and Genetics of ADHD," Internet Special Education Resources. www.iser.com/resources/genetics-ADHD.html.

Barbara Kantrowitz and Anne Underwood, "Dyslexia and the New Science of Reading," *Newsweek*, January 31, 2000.

Stephanie Lindsley, "Autism and Education," *Newsweek*, February 28, 2009.

Krista Mahr, "ADHD Kids Can Get Better," *Time*, November 12, 2007.

Liza Mundy, "Success Is in Her DNA," *Washington Post*, October 20, 2009.

Tiffany O'Callaghan, "Dyslexia in Different Languages," *Time,* October 13, 2009.

Tara Parker-Pope, "New Face for A.D.H.D., and a Debate," *New York Times,* November 24, 2008.

Karen Plumley, "Children with Writing Disabilities," Suite101 .com, January 25, 2010. http://specialneedseducation.suite101 .com/article.cfm/children_with_writing_disabilities.

Steven Schulman, "Facing the Invisible Handicap," *Psychology Today,* vol. 2, 1986.

Sally S. Scott, "Accommodating Students with Learning Disabilities: How Much Is Enough?" *Innovative Higher Education,* vol. 22, 1997.

H. Silver-Pacuilla, "Getting Started with Assistive Technology," *Focus on Basics,* vol. 8, Issue D, 2007.

Kristin Stanberry and Marshall H. Raskind, "Assistive Technology for Kids with Learning Disabilities: An Overview," Reading Rockets.org, 2009. www.readingrockets.org/article/33074.

Anne Underwood, "New Clues to the Puzzle of Dyslexia," *Newsweek,* June 7, 1999.

Francisco Vara-Orta, "Boy Is Empowered by His Weakness," *Los Angeles Times,* January 7, 2008.

INDEX